Advanced Digital Data Security Using Blockchain and Cryptographic Techniques

Rodger Smith

CHAPTER - 1
INTRODUCTION

CONTENTS

1.1 Overview

Digital data security holds vital importance in today's rapidly changing and digitalised world, with the advent of new technologies. As digital technology and the Internet have advanced, there is a greater need than ever to secure both personal and business information. With information security breaches on the rise and cyber attacks becoming increasingly sophisticated, digital data security awareness has become a crucial issue for individuals. The scope of digital security encompasses understanding online threats, knowing how to defend against them, and actively using these defences across all devices. Protecting users' digital data starts with the creation of strong passwords and continues with the use of both free and paid security tools. Digital information security is of great importance at both the organisational and individual levels. Financial losses, reputational harm, and legal punishments are just a few of the severe repercussions that may result from information loss or unauthorised access. In terms of people's security and privacy, protecting personal information is very important. For this reason, digital information security has become an increasingly important and widespread area today [1].

1.2 Rise of Digital Ecosystems

From an ecological point of view, one of the best definitions of "Digital Ecosystem" is given in[2]: "A Digital Ecosystem is a network of interconnected digital resources, including but not limited to software, data, services, contracts, laws, training modules, business models and procedures, expertise, and more." An element may be deemed digital if it can be formalised or naturally articulated in a language, then transferred digitally within an ecosystem, and has the ability to be processed by either people or computers. The components of the Digital Ecosystem may be described, composed, evolved, integrated, shared, and distributed thanks to its infrastructure. In terms of economics, the Digital Ecosystem is defined in [3] as "a helpful model for comprehending the interplay between regional and sectoral business networks and information and communication technologies". "An innovative strategy for accelerating SME-driven, environmentally responsible regional development is digital ecosystems," says the OPAALS project community, introducing the concept of a Digital Ecosystem[4].

This technology operates in a shared worldwide public environment and is distributed and peer-to-peer." The Digital Ecosystem is seen from a technological perspective as the digital equivalent of biological ecosystems, which are believed to be scalable, highly resilient, and self-organising systems capable of independently resolving complex, dynamic issues. The definitions presented above provide different viewpoints on the Digital Ecosystem. Nonetheless, it is important to examine digital ecosystems from a multidisciplinary and comprehensive standpoint[5]: "A digital ecosystem is an autonomous network of interconnected digital resources with the goal of fostering collaboration, information exchange, the growth of flexible and open technology, and the creation of business models." Nonetheless, the Digital Ecosystem is universally abstracted in this description.

1.3 Challenges of Traditional Security Models

Traditional security models have long relied on centralised architectures, particularly through the use of Public Key Infrastructure (PKI) and Certificate Authorities (CAs), to manage identity authentication, data integrity, and secure communication. However, both contemporary reviews and empirical research have highlighted a growing list of limitations inherent in these centralised approaches.

- **Single Point of Failure**

Centralised security models concentrate trust in third-party authorities such as CAs. The system as a whole is vulnerable to a potential breach of the trusted authority due to the setup's one weak spot.[6]extensively reviewed global PKI infrastructures and demonstrated multiple vulnerabilities that allow attackers to forge certificates or misuse validation paths. The case of the Digi Notar compromise serves as a real-world example, wherein the issuance of fraudulent certificates led to a systemic breakdown of digital trust [7].

- **Latency and Scalability Bottlenecks**

The centralized nature of traditional systems outcome resulted in latency during key issuance and certificate validation, particularly in large-scale and distributed environments. [8]studied identity management solutions in depth and found that conventional centralised PKIs have trouble scaling effectively across IoT ecosystems because it must constantly communicate with a centralised validation authority. Applications in the real world, like smart grids and edge computing, that depend on low latency would be negatively affected by this obstacle.

- **Key Mismanagement and Operational Risks**

Reviews of key management practices, as summarized in NIST Special Publication 800-57 (2020), reveal that human error in key issuance, storage, renewal, or revocation remains a significant vulnerability. Cryptographic keys handlers' Cryptographic keys are frequently manipulated and misconfigured manually, leading to certificate expiry or inappropriate access controls that can be used by an attacker. These are operational dangers that are more pronounced in an environment devoid of automated key lifecycle management systems.

- **Regulatory and Compliance Inflexibility**

The transparency and the adaptability of traditional PKI systems are criticized more and more as global laws on data protection change. GDPR and CCPA compliance research[9]suggests that centralized trust models are ill-equipped to offer the fine-grained access, control, consent management, and audit ability requested in contemporary approaches to data governance. This strictness prevents compliance and can cause the organizations to be exposed to regulatory fines and reputation damages.

- **Public Key Infrastructure (PKI) Breaches and Trust Erosion**

Various scholars have examined the historical pitfalls of CAs and the drawbacks of PKI environments. [10]asserted that centralities models of trust are becoming obsolete on repeated violations and growing system complexities. The faith of the global community in CAs was shaken by mis-issued certificates by the likes of Symantec and Comodo and also by a failure of revocation procedures.

1.4 Emergence of Integrated Security Frameworks

The dynamic nature of cyber security demands strong and decentralized systems to protect digital assets, especially in cases where digital records and online transactions grow. The challenges we are faced with in terms of modern distributed environments are starting to overtake the traditional and centralized types of security models. The identification of such drawbacks has led to the development of a favourable alternative: the convergence of the blockchain, sophisticated cryptography, and self-signed keys so that the combination results in a security system.

1.4.1 Blockchain technology

The decentralised trust and transparency that Blockchain Technology offers is built upon. Blockchain, a distributed and immutable ledger, ensures the data authenticity, verifiability, and integrity with no reliance on a single focal point. Using consensus methods to validate each transaction, such as Proof of Work (PoW) or Proof of Stake (PoS), removes the possibility of a centralised breach or single point of failure[11]. Its uses as a healthcare records security measure [12], the Supply Chain system, and the used in digital identity management[13]demonstrate its potential to become a fundamental security infrastructure.

1.4.2 Cryptographic techniques

The use of cryptography, especially the use of public-key cryptography offers both in-transit and rest data encryption and therefore offers safe communications and data confidentiality. Later more advanced methods include homomorphic encryption, ECC and ZKPs that offer greater efficiency and guarantees of privacy. Used in contexts of blockchain based systems, it provide privacy in combination with transparency, and verifiability[14].

1.4.3 Self-signed keys

Self-signed keys, commonly considered to be at an insecure disadvantage in classical PKI systems due to the lack of third-party validation, are a key component in the decentralized context of security. These enable individuals or entities to create, share and control their own public/private key pairs without a need to rely on certificate authorities (CAs). It eradicates the reliance on centralized infrastructures of trust that in the past have been prone to hacking and certificate issuance errors. In blockchain communities, self-sovereign identity (SSI) systems use self-signed keys to place the user in charge of their digital credentials[15].

The convergence of these three domains, blockchain, cryptography, and self-signed keys, forms a cohesive, decentralized security architecture. Such frameworks ensure the authenticity, confidentiality, and integrity of digital records across dynamic, multi-user systems. There are particularly relevant in contexts like e-health, financial services, and digital governance, where sensitive information must be protected against evolving threats and unauthorized access[16]

1.5 Blockchain Technology in Digital Data Security

1.5.1 Historical Overview of Blockchain

The digital transformation that blockchain technology has brought about has been most profound in the domain of papers, contracts, and transactions; these being the bedrock of our society's economic, social, and political systems. An mysterious programmer going by the name of Satoshi Nakamoto launched Bitcoin in 2008, ushering in the first generation of blockchain technology. This laid the groundwork for blockchain technology and signalled the introduction of cryptocurrency into monetary-based financial applications like digital payment systems. Smart contracts, an element of the 2nd generation blockchain, enabled the technology to be used for purposes beyond monetary transactions, including smart property, loans, and stocks[17]. The use of third-generation blockchain technology has expanded beyond the banking and financial sectors to include the public sector, education, and healthcare. New BlockchainTechnology has emerged in less than a decade, promising to integrate digital intelligence with AI. An excellent indication of the technology's surprising popularity and development is the fact that in 2010, Laszlo Hanyecz spent 10,000 bitcoins on two $30 PapaJohn's pizzas. Predictions for the value of these bitcoins in 2018 exceeded $80 million. This exemplifies the meteoric rise of digital currency and related technologies.

1.5.2 Blockchain Structure and Operation

The distributed ledger technology called "blockchain" employs a system of interconnected computers to permanently record transactions with a timestamp and no human intervention. Figure 1.1 shows the procedures involved in the functioning of blockchain. The five-step process that describes how blockchain works is as follows:

- **Transaction Request-** The safe and verifiable storing of data is at the heart of smart contracts. A successful completion of the sender-receiver transaction is guaranteed by the transaction request. The information on the Bitcoin blockchain is only relevant to Bitcoin transactions, which fall under the category of financial information. From the initial Bitcoin transaction to the present, this is an exhaustive record of every financial transaction.
- **Chaining the Blocks-** An interconnection among nodes in a P2P network is established once the data for the transaction request is established. The process entails linking and chaining the blocks together to create a single entity. In Figure 1.1, four blocks are chained together, each containing transaction data.

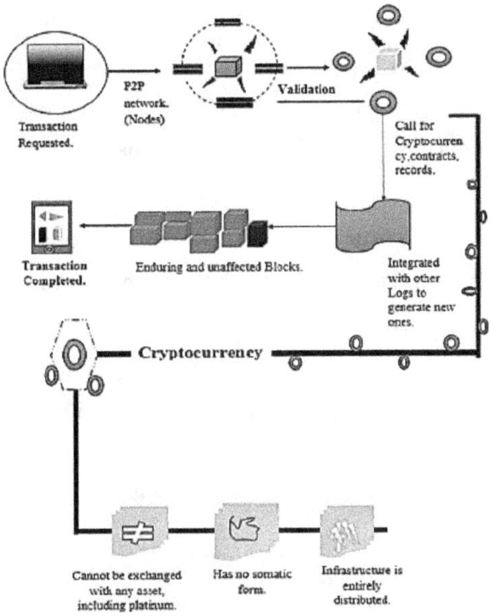

Figure 1.1: Working of blockchain

- **Validation:** Blockchain decouples block validation from chaining and necessitates verification for validation. Hashing and cryptocurrency technology are prepared to use all blocks. A confirmation of funds is required prior to any disbursement. Many additional public information papers, such those from the public library or the Securities and Exchange

Commission, have a person responsible for looking for newly uploaded materials. The assignment is now assigned to a computer network using blockchain. While making an Amazon purchase, the system checks to see whether the money went through as you said it would[18].The steps involved in the blockchain's operation are laid forth in Figure 1.2.

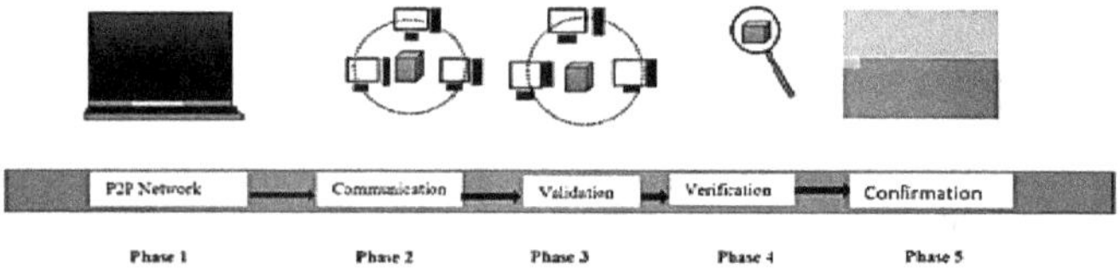

Figure 1.2: Phase-wise procedure of the processes of blockchain.

- **Digital Signature and Hashing:** Digital signatures and hashes are required for each block at this point since all blocks are requesting cryptocurrency contact details. The use of Digital Signatures verifies that funds are going to the correct owners in transactions, and hashing ensures that everyone on the blockchain is in agreement on the current state of things. These are crucial factors of blockchain that guarantee its integrity and prevent corruption.
- **Integration Operations:** The integration process involves joining all blocks to the logs. It gets the ideal justification after verifying the payment is accurate. The digital signatures of the buyer, Amazon, and the total amount of the transaction make up most of the file. A large number of these entities—tens to millions—are likely to be included in the payment here.
  Figure 1.2 shows the five stages that make up a blockchain process.

These steps are listed below:

- Phase 1– P2P network
- Phase 2– Communication
- Phase 3– Validation
- Phase 4– Verification
- Phase 5– Confirmation

1.5.3 Types of Blockchain

Blockchain technology is finding usage in private networks and other applications. It ensures that authorised users are the only ones who may access protected information. In this scenario, the only people who can oversee the operations are the network administrators. Those administrators must be contacted by any node or user wishing to get access to the network. There are two primary ways to classify Blockchain technology: private and public[19]. Blockchain technology goes by many names than just that; consortium blockchain and hybrid blockchain are two more that emerge from different analyses and criteria. A cluster of nodes running on a P2P network technology is fundamental to every blockchain type. In order to authorise, initiate, and verify transactions, each node in the network maintains its own copy of the shared ledger, which is updated in real-time[20]. Experts have categorised Blockchain Technology into three main areas, taking into consideration its expansive nature:

- Public Blockchain,
- Private Blockchain,

1.5.3.1 Public Blockchain

A prominent kind of Blockchain, known as public blockchain, is both publicly accessible and decentralised. The networks that facilitate transactions using this Blockchain Technology are basically accessible to everybody interested. Furthermore, two varieties of PoW and PoS models are in use, with the validated person effectively receiving the transaction rewards [21].Furthermore, there is no permission required for the Public Blockchain, which is a distributed, non-restrictive ledger system. The data or a section of the Blockchain may be made available to anybody with access. The ability to authorise the confirmation of both past and current data is another characteristic of this blockchain type. Many are also utilising it to mine and sell cryptocurrencies. There are a lot of blockchains out there, but the two most dominant ones are Bitcoin and Litecoin[22]. It is mostly secure when followed strictly and adhered to security rules and methods. Nonetheless, there is a potential danger in disregarding security standards. This kind of Blockchain is shown, for instance, by

- Bitcoin
- Ethereum
- Litecoin

The benefits and distinguishing characteristics of public Blockchain systems are shown in Figure 1.3.

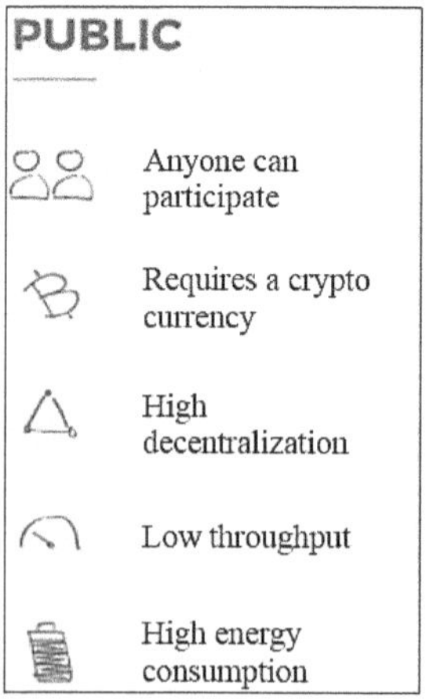

Figure 1.3: Salient features and functions of the public blockchains

According to experts[23]two typical instances of PublicBlockchains are as follows: Bitcoin and Ethereum [21]. The aspects that this Blockchain type is focused on are viz.

- High Security and Privacy,
- Open and Flexible Environment,
- Anonymous Nature,
- No Regulations and strict Policies,
- Full Transparency and Systems.
- Distributed, etc.

1.5.3.2 Private blockchains

In addition to having access control methods, private blockchains are closed and not publicly accessible. The system administrator may facilitate permitted transactions using this blockchain type[24]. The following features are inherent to the platforms developed by private blockchain solutions.

- Full of privacy
- High efficiency
- Faster transaction
- Better scalability
- Faster and speediness

Networks and systems with restricted access to a limited number of approved users, such those in for-profit and non-profit companies, are ideal for this blockchain design. The accessibility, authorisation, permissions, and security of this blockchain type are all top priorities. The experts say that private blockchains are used for a lot of different things, such voting, managing SupplyChains, verifying digital identities, and keeping track of assets. Multichain, Hyperledger projects, and Corda are just a few of the well-known private blockchains. The key characteristics and uses of private blockchains are shown in Figure 1.4.

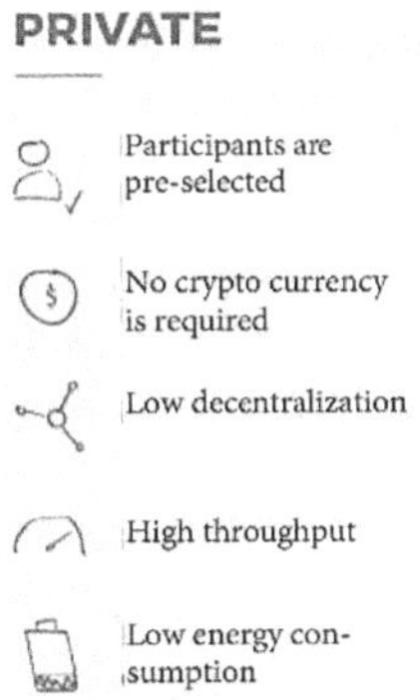

Figure 1.4: Salient features and functions of the private blockchains.

Data exchanged between nodes in a private blockchain cannot be seen by anybody outside of the private network as only authorised nodes may execute transactions. The figure 1.5 displays the Types of Blockchains and roadmaps.

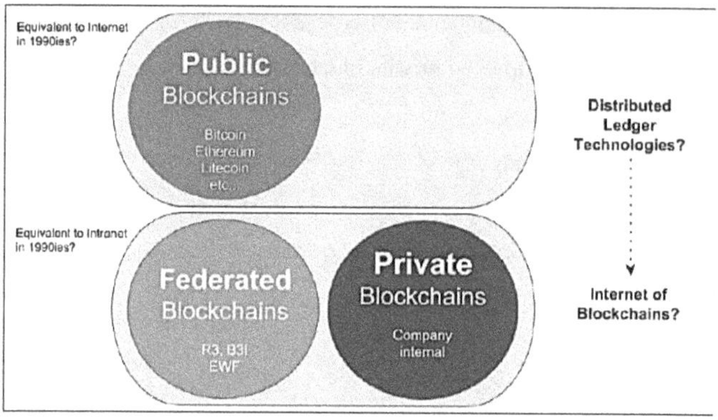

Figure 1.5: Types of Blockchains and roadmaps

The activities of both public and private blockchains are generally regarded as advantageous or remarkable, and each blockchain has a unique set of benefits (Figure 1.6). The expert believes that the most crucial and vital features of both public and private blockchains are security, scalability, and transparency. It should be noted that public networks are crucial in PoW-based systems, whereas private blockchains are unreliable[25].

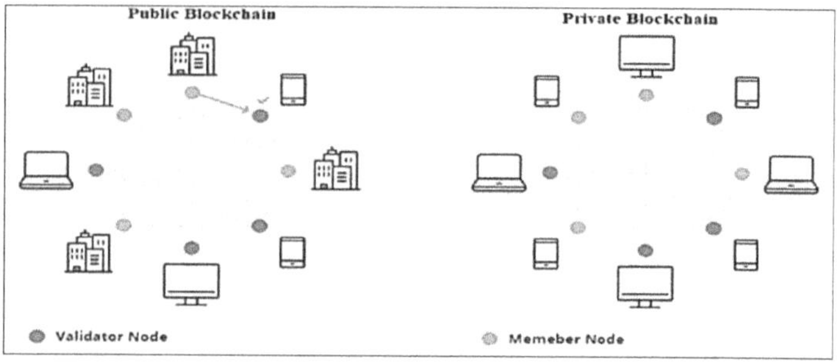

Figure 1.6: Architecture-wise differences in public and private blockchains.

1.6 Key Attributes of Blockchain Technology

1.6.1 Decentralisation

Centralisation and decentralisation are utterly distinct concepts. Compared to centralised apps, it provides more security and flexibility. Decentralisation has been embraced by several companies due to the need for quick decision-making[26]. Everything is done in one place in a concentrated setting. A decentralised ecosystem may foster creativity and efficiency when it operates in several places. Efficiency aims to provide better outcomes by reducing expenses and time. Innovation generates a new concept. That ought to be a new advantage.Figure 1.7 shows the network comparison graphs.

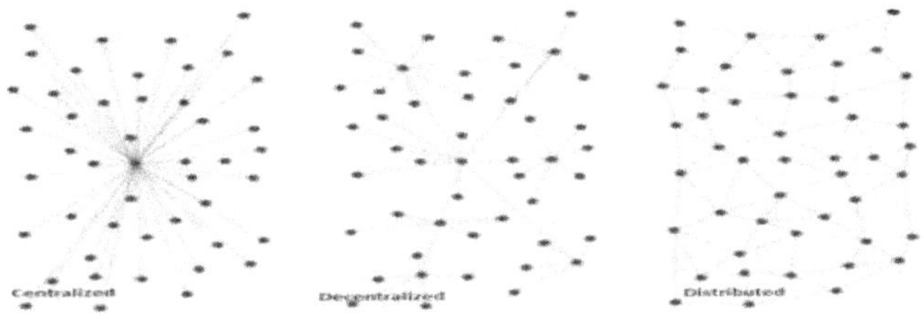

Figure 1.7: Network Comparison

- **Trust:** Blockchain technology establishes a connection between the data included in one block and the data contained in the previous block. Authentication will be facilitated during the transaction by means of this. Nothing is communicated with by outside parties. It will instead make use of a public ledger. It is expected that all transactions would be logged automatically in this ledger.
- **Transparent:** Data recorded in a blockchain is both visible and unchangeable. Trust in blockchains is based on this reason[27].

1.6.2 Use Cases in Digital Data Security

1. Healthcare

The healthcare business places a high priority on the security of patient information. Systems built on the blockchain provide decentralised and immutable ways to store EHRs. Self-signed key mechanisms can help patients and practitioners securely control access to medical data without relying on third-party certificate authorities[28]. These technologies will ensure that no one other than a doctor or insurance company, who has authorisation, may see or change a patient's record. This level of access granularity has the effect of preserving privacy as well as facilitate the adherence to privacy laws regarding health data protection such as HIPAA[29]. Moreover, immutability of blockchain contributes to all changes to health records stored forever with time-stamped audit trails which increases accountability and allows safe telemedicine and the transmission of data across hospitals.

2. Finance

Security, traceability and transparency are not negotiable in financial systems. The decentralised ledger provided by Blockchain provides an effective means to secure financial transactions, control risk, and ensure regulatory compliance[30]. The ability to record each transaction in a cryptographically secured and immutable ledger helps financial institutions to avoid unauthorised access, fraudulent transactions and full exposure of audit trails. The strategy is in line with the requirements of international regulatory authorities to comply with regulations[31]. Self-signed keys allow institutions to create their own identities, sign transactions without the involvement of centralised Certificate Authorities (CAs), and mitigate risks that key mismanagement poses and single points of failure.

1.6.3 E-Governance

Governments globally are adopting digital systems for public service delivery, necessitating secure and transparent mechanisms for identity verification, document authentication, and voting systems. Blockchain technology offers a reliable infrastructure for tamper-proof digital identities, which can be used for accessing e-services, tax filing, subsidy claims, or welfare distribution[32].For electoral processes, blockchain-based voting ensures end-to-end verifiability, voter anonymity, and resistance to tampering. Votes are irrevocable once cast due to blockchain's decentralised nature, which removes reliance on a central authority [33]. Smart contracts can also automate decision-making in public procurement and legal processes, increasing trust and efficiency in governance.

1.6.4 Challenges in Blockchain

Blockchain has encountered certain difficulties in the business world, particularly when it comes to Bitcoin transactions. These issues are listed below and are fundamental to the way the Bitcoin blockchain operates. outlines a few common difficulties below.

- **Scalability**

Every day, more transactions are being made.Blockchain is being recommended by the majority of businesses for their transaction operations. Every transaction must be recorded and confirmed. The block will have a very limited capacity. The preference of miners for high transaction fees necessitates the postponement of some transactions. The propagation speed will thus decrease due to the greater block size[34]. The scalability issue is thus quite serious. The scalability issue with blockchain may be avoided in a few ways.

- Storage Optimization of blockchain
- Redesigning blockchain

1. Privacy Leakage

Users felt that blockchain provides a higher level of anonymity when dealing with sensitive information. A user's identity could not be stored in blockchain; just their address could be. Blockchain is not able to provide global privacy, as shown by Meiklejohn (2013) and Kosba (2016). Bitcoin transactions may be traced back to a user's identity by using their account address, according to recent research. Identity leaks were occurring as an outcome of the issues. A solution to this issue exists in the form of EllipticCurveDiffie-HellmanMerkle (ECDHM). The topic of public and private keys will be covered[35]. This will facilitate the exchange of confidential information between two individuals. It will facilitate the encryption of internet message transactions. A secure platform, like Ethereum and smart contracts, is also created to ensure the security of transactions.

2. MITM Attack

"Man in the middle attack" is abbreviated as MITM. Third party contact describes this. A user stepped in the middle here, and it's possible that their public key is fake. The sensitive data may be simply decrypted by him using this key. A blockchain network's nodes are each given a public key. A block should be connected to both the block before it and the block after it [36]. This prevents the use of a forged key to change or compromise the PublicKey.

3. DDoS Attack

An assault called a DDoSattack is directed against a specific system, such a computer, website, server, or other network resource. Consequently, the target system's incoming messages or connections may lag, crash, or even shut down. In blockchain, in particular, a DDoS assault poses a serious danger to company[37]. This sort of assault is very hard to avoid.

1.7 Cryptography-Based Algorithms for Enhanced Security

Information may be securely stored and hidden from intruders using cryptography, allowing only authorised users to view and distribute the information as intended.Encryption, cryptography, and authentication techniques help reduce security risks[38]. The field of cryptography focusses on the secure generation of messages that alter data during transmission by encrypting plaintext using user input and then executing a reverse decryption technique that restores the original text[39]. The key way to safeguard sensitive data is encryption, and cryptography can fix problems with cloud computing's network data and application security. Protecting information from prying eyes is cryptography's main goal. A new and exciting field of research, symmetric-key cryptography has arisen in the rapidly developing field of encryption. The term "symmetric key encryption" describes a method of encryption and decryption that uses the same key. An enormous amount of data will be encrypted since it can be processed quickly with only one key."[40]. There is currently no standard operating procedure in place to safeguard data stored by cloud service providers from unauthorised access or other types of attack. The cloud employs a cryptographic mechanism that makes it difficult for the attacker to decipher the ciphertext, protecting end-user data from cyber threats. A longer key is more secure than a shorter one since it makes deciphering the encrypted content difficult.

1.7.1 Term used in Cryptography

An important part of cryptography is the use of mathematical expressions to convert data from plaintext (P) to ciphertext (C), which is unreadable. The procedure is known as encryption, and it involves a collection of methods called

CryptographicAlgorithms (E) and a DecryptionAlgorithm (D) that inverts and creates[41]. The way this is characterised is

- Cipher-text (C= E {P, Key}
- Plain-text (C = D {C, Key}

An explanation of a few key terms used in encryption:

- Plain text is the first input or data presented to coding procedures from an intuitive source.
- The result of encoding a MixedMessage into an indecipherable stream of characters is called the cypher text.
- Encryption algorithm approaches substitute and modify plain text to create encrypted content in the encryption process.
- The encrypted text may be restored to its original state by using a decryption technique in reverse, which entails employing the encryption key.
- Keys: There are the building blocks of an encryption or decryption algorithm.
- Senders and receivers: These people communicate and exchange text messages on a regular basis.

Data, communication, file systems, and host systems are all vulnerable to new security threats brought forth by cloud computing. Encryption may enable organisations temporarily overcome these concerns and use cloud computing [42].

The primary goal of implementing cryptography is to meet the following fundamental standards for data protection:

- Confidentiality "Unauthorised disclosure of private information is something it aims to prevent. An increase in the potential for unauthorised disclosure is a side effect of cloud storage's accessibility across a variety of devices and applications" [43].Thus, methods like encryption[44]must be utilized to safeguard the data stored in the cloud.
- Integrity "A security of cloud Data Management relies on it, as it prevents data from being altered or deleted without authorisation." This is a huge issue with the current authorisation systems on the cloud[45]. Every

authenticated account's access rights are defined by the authorisation, which limits unauthorised users. However, it is crucial to guarantee that only allowed companies may access sensitive data due to the increasing number of both access points and device entities.

- Availability term "cloud computing" encompasses not just data and programs but also storage on a remote server environment that authorised users may access whenever necessary it. A cloud infrastructure's ability to continue operations in the face of misbehaviour by other authorities is crucial to efficiency [42].
- Authorization this requires figuring out who can use what kinds of data and resources on the computer. The foundation of all administrative practises and fundamental operations is it. The policies outline the terms and circumstances under which data and computer resources may be accessed[46].
- Non-repudiations it denotes the entitlement to ensure that the originator of a communication or document cannot contest the authenticity of its signature or transmission. To put it another way, a sender shouldn't have to refute that he got a communication afterward[47].

Numerous more secure ways are available in cryptography, and it is feasible to use these approaches after deliver these security services. Tools like hash functions, digital signatures, and encryption protocols fall within this category.

- **Symmetric Algorithms** "Symmetric (public key) keys are used only in cryptography; The majority of SymmetricKeyAlgorithms encrypt and decode data employing a single standard key ("DES", "TripleDES", "RivestCipher 4 (RC4)", "International DataEncryptionAlgorithm (IDEA)", and "AES") [48].
- **Asymmetric Algorithms:**Public key cryptography also uses them in AsymmetricKey cryptography, which uses 2 keys for encryption and decryption. Various Asymmetric Algorithms, also called private key algorithms, are available, including "RSA," "ElGamal," "Diffie-Hellman," and so on.
- **Hybrid Algorithms:**A technique for encrypting data that combines many algorithms is called hybrid encryption. In simpler terms, it entails re-

encoding a document that has already been encrypted using one or more techniques, either identically or differently. Using several encryption methods is made simple by encryption and decryption[49].

1.7.2 Types of Cryptography

Symmetric Key Cryptography: Data encryption and decryption in Symmetric Key cryptography (also called SecretKeyCryptography) are accomplished via the use of a Single Key. Prior to transmitting data using SymmetricKeyCryptography, the SecretKey is determined. The communication begins with the sender sending the ciphertext to the recipient after encrypting the plaintext using the key. Data may be accessed, decoded, and the plaintext obtained by the receiver using the same SecretKey[50]. The algorithms AES, DES, T-DES, E-DES, RC6, Two Fish, Serpent, and Blowfish are examples of symmetric encryption. Figure 1.8 depicts the SymmetricKeyCryptography encryption and decryption process.

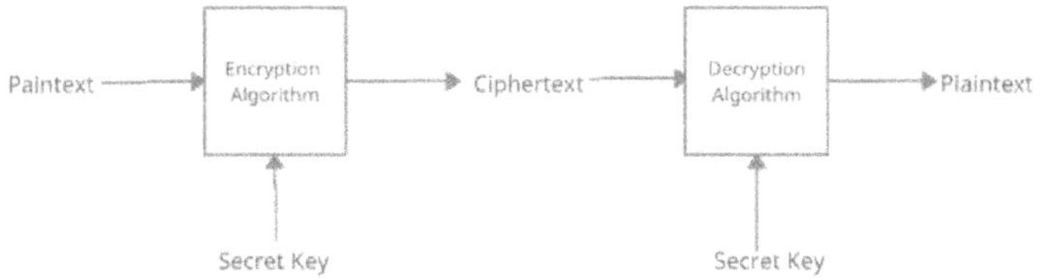

Figure 1.8: Process of Encryption and decryption in symmetric key cryptography.

Asymmetric Key Cryptography: AsymmetricKeyCryptography (sometimes called PublicKey cryptography) and PrivateKey cryptography both rely on distinct keys. A PublicKey and a PrivateKey, which together make up an asymmetric key pair, are utilized for encryption and decryption. It is possible to get the PublicKey with asymmetric cryptography by first acquiring the private key, and vice versa. It should only be the owner who has permission to use the private key[51]. Asymmetric Encryption Algorithm includes ECC, RSA, EES, DigitalSecure, and Diffie-Hellman. An illustration of the asymmetric key cryptography encryption and decryption process is displayed in Figure 1.9.

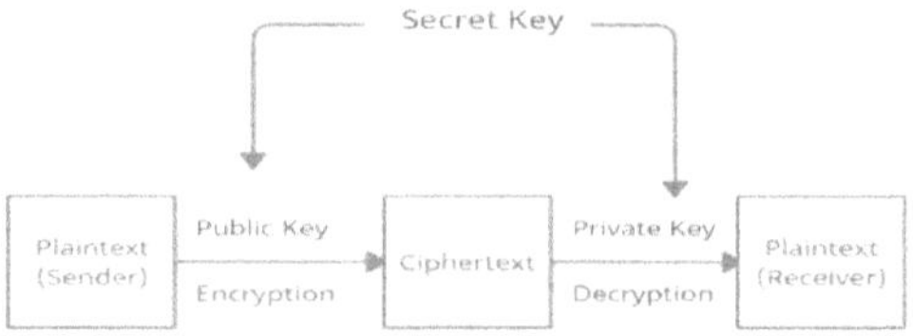

Figure 1.9: Process of Encryption and decryption in Asymmetric key cryptography.

Hash Functions: Hash functions are not key-dependent and are one-way functions. The hashing method can't be used to retrieve the original data since it converts it to a value of a certain length. Since the hashing process always produces the same result for the same plaintext, cracking a hash requires trying every conceivable input until the exact same hash is discovered. One way to compare passwords without keeping them is by using hashing[52]. Among the many hash functions are NTLM, LANMAN, MD5, SHA-1, and SHA-2.

1.7.3 Cryptography Algorithms

A. Data Encryption Standard (DES)

The DES is a BlockCypher that uses a Symmetric Key and a subkey of 48 bits to generate a cipher text of 64 bits from an encrypted plaintext of 64 bits. Decryption and encryption in DES share a single secret key. The DES makes use of the Feistel Cypher, which requires a 16-round Feistel structure.[53]The default key length is 64 bits. After removing 8 superfluous keys, the real key length is 56 bits. Then, it splits the 56-bit key in half, with each half containing 28 bits.

These are the steps that make up DES:

- An Initial Permutation (IP) function is the first to receive a 64-bit plaintext block.
- The plaintext is encrypted using the IP.
- LeftPlainText (LPT) and RightPlainText (RPT) are the two components of the permuted block that are created in the first permutation
- After then, there are a total of sixteen rounds of encryption for both the LPT and the RPT.

- After everything is re-joined, the LPT and RPT blocks go through one more Final Permutation (FP).
- At last, this procedure produces 64-bit ciphertext.

B. Advanced Encryption Standard (AES)

Figure 1.10 displayed that the AES is officially called the Rijndael Algorithm. It employs Symmetric Block cyphers with key sizes of 128/192/256 bits to encrypt data in 128-bit blocks. In the initial stage, it uses a 16-byte 4x4 matrix to store data in a single block; in subsequent stages, it expands to employ multiple keys for each rounds based on an SP network topology[54]. The AES takes a text message as input, transforms it into a block, and then uses that block to create a state array.

The steps in AES are:

- **Add round key:** The Block Data kept in the state array and the initial key created throughout the procedure are combined using an XOR operation.
- **Sub-Bytes:** Rows and columns of the Final State array are updated with the new values using a substitution box (S-Box) after the state is divided in half and each byte is converted to hexadecimal.
- **Shift Rows:** The state rows are shifted cyclically throughout this permutation phase. The first row is skipped, followed by a one-byte leftward shift of the second row, a two-byte leftward shift of the third row, and a three-place leftward shift of the last row.
- **Mix Columns:** The "Mix Columns" linear procedure takes each column in the current array and multiplies a constant matrix with it to generate a new column for the next state array. A whole new 16-byte matrix is produced by merging the columns.
- **Add round key:** The 16-byte matrix is XORed with its corresponding key, making it 128 bits long. This either generates the Ciphertext for that specific block or feeds it into the new state array for the next round.

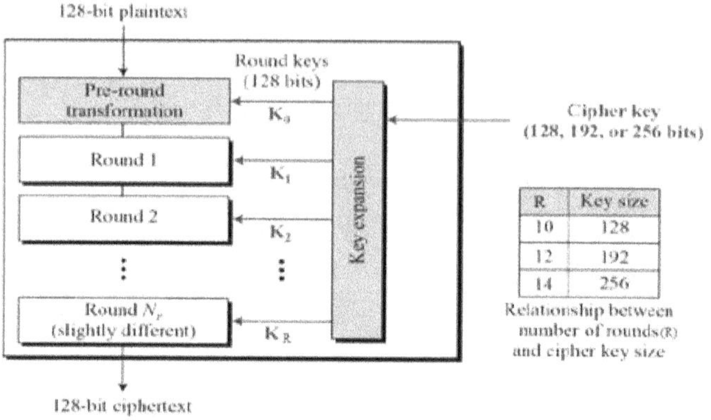

Figure 1.10: AES Structure.

C. Elliptic Curve Cryptography (ECC)

ECC employs a PublicKey cryptography technique for data security. Public and private keys are both supported by ECC for data encryption and decryption. It is possible to generate digital signatures using the PrivateKey and then verify their authenticity with the PublicKey.ECC is superior to RSA since it uses fewer keys to offer the same security level. An ECCkey with 384 bits, for instance, may provide the same degree of security as an RSAkey with 7680 bits[55].

- RSA key length – 1024 2048 3072 7680 15360 in bits
- ECC key length – 160 224 256 384 521 in bits

Elliptic curve theory, which explores an algebraic structure of elliptic curves over finite fields, is the foundation of the ECC approach, which offers more security than RSA. Keys generated by ECC are therefore more challenging to solve theoretically. The following equation describes the ECC, which is a planar and asymmetrical curve that passes across a finite field: y^2 = x^3+ax+b. The Elliptic Curve theory over finite fields is the basis of a number of algorithms made available by ECC:

- The EllipticCurveDigital Signature Algorithm (ECDSA) and the Edwards-curve Digital Signature Algorithm (EdDSA), both of which use classical curves, are examples of ECC digital signature algorithms.

- ECIES and EEECC (EC-based ElGamal) are two examples of hybrid encryption methods that use ECC techniques.
- An elliptic curve Diffie-Hellman key exchange utilising curve22519, FullyHashedMenezes-Qu-Vanstone (FHMQV), and Elliptic Curve Diffie-Hellman (ECDH) are all examples of ECC key agreement procedures. The figure 1.11 shows the ECC Structure.

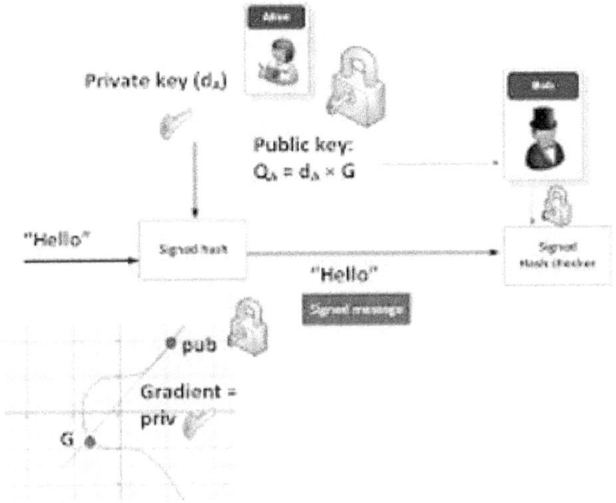

Figure 1.11: ECC Structure.

D. Rivest-Shamir-Adleman (RSA)

The RSA technique is an example of PublicKeyCryptography, which uses 2 distinct but mathematically related keys—a PublicKey and a PrivateKey—to encrypt and decode data. With RSA, you may use the public or PrivateKey to encrypt a message. A two keys, one for encryption and one for decryption, function identically whether the keys are public or private. With RSA, factoring a big number becomes a real challenge. Since both the PublicKey and the PrivateKey are composed of two prime integers, the greater of the two may be factored to reveal the compromised private key. As a result, encryption strength is proportional to key size, and it grows exponentially with key size. Numbers between zero and n-1 (for some n) constitute RSA's plaintext and ciphertext[56]. The usual value of n is 309 decimal digits, or

1024 bits, which means that n is less than 2^1024. The figure 1.12 shows the RSA algorithm structure.

The three-step process that RSA follows is as follows:

- **Key Generation**
  - Choose x and y, two bigger prime integers.
  - Calculate n=x*y,where n is the encryption and decryption modulus.
  - Determine the totient functionPhi(n) = (x-1) * (y-1)
  - Select the PublicKey exponent e in a way that 1<e<Phi(n) e is prime to Phi(n) i.e. GCD(e,Phi(n)) =1
  - Determine the PrivateKey exponent d in a way that e*d=1*mod (Phi(n)). Thus, PublicKey: (n,e) PrivateKey: (n,d)
- **Encryption:** To encrypt a communication, one must first send plain text to the recipient using the PublicKey (n,e). C = P^e mod(n)
- **Decryption:** APrivateKey (n,d), a plaintext is P = c^d mod(n)

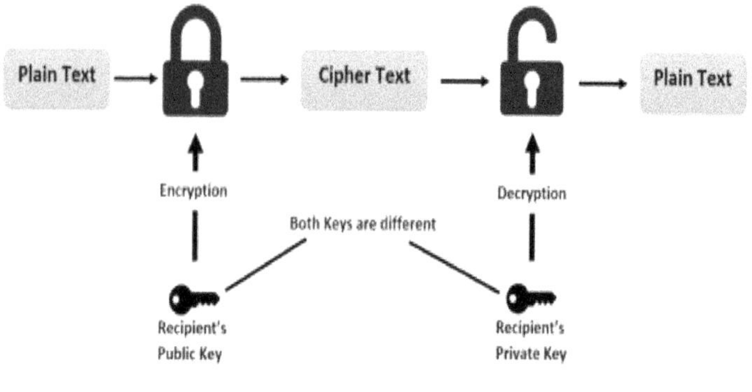

Figure 1.12: RSA Structure.

E. Blowfish

An alternative to DES or IDEA is the 64-bit symmetric block cypher known as Blowfish. Its key-length can be adjusted between 32 bits and 448 bits. The encryption method and the protection of sensitive data are both made possible by Blowfish, a 16-round structure. Encryption takes a 64-bit plaintext as input and produces a 64-bit ciphertext using the same secret key.

It is structured like the Feistel network and has four distinct steps to complete an operation:

- **Key expansion:** A maximum of 448 bits is possible, with 32 bits being the minimum. Several sub-key arrays, totalling 4168 bytes, are created from a key of around 448 bits throughout the process. The P-array has 18 32-bit entries, while the S-boxes each have 32 bits and hold 256 items, making them two sub-key arrays.
- **Data Encryption:** The technique iteratively traverses the network sixteen times throughout the data encryption process. The Blowfish algorithm is a lightning-fast cipher-text generator.
- **Key Generation:** A plethora of sub-keys are produced by blowfish[57].

The key sizes of the 18 sub-keys that make up a P-array vary from 32 bits all the way up to 448bits, or 14words.

4 S-boxes consist of 256entries of 32bits.

- **Steps to generate Sub-keys:** It is recommended to initialise the P-array before proceeding to initialise 4 S-boxes with a Fixed String. There are a few more hexadecimal digits than the first three in this string that make up pi. Following an initialisation of XOR P1 with the first 32bits of the key, the remaining 320bits of the key are XORed with XOR P2. This process must be repeated until the key bits of the P-array have been XORed. Figure 1.13 shows the Blowfish structure.

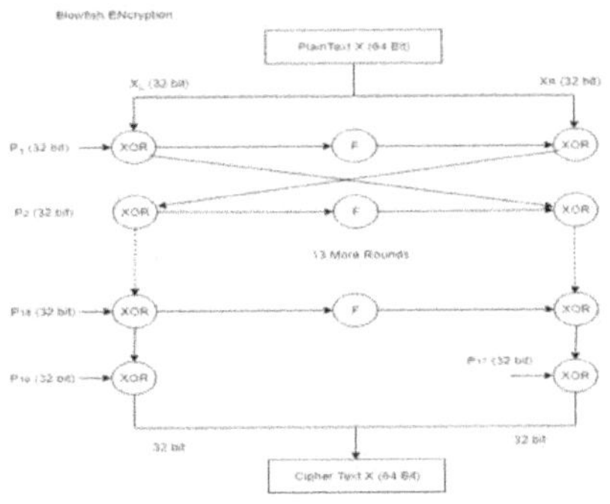

Figure 1.13: Blowfish structure.

F. Message Direct Algorithm (MD5)

The MD5 algorithm is a cryptographic one-way function that converts strings of arbitrary length into 128-bit values, which are then converted into 32-digit hexadecimal integers. By padding each message into a block of 512 bits, MD5 verifies the validity of the sent text. The procedure continues to the final block, with each block doing 16 operations across 4 rounds for a total of 64 operations. The next block then receives the output from the previous block. The direct message is the output of the final block. Its primary use case is in public key cryptosystems for digital signatures, where a secret key is utilized to encrypt a compressed version of a bigger file [58]. This is the sequence of operations that make up the MD5 algorithm:

- **Append Padding Bits**: The input quantity should be 64 bits less than a multiple of 512 when it is received. A single character is appended at the outset of the padding, and the remaining characters are zeros to provide additional characters.
- **Append Length Bits:** Put the 64-bit message together by adding length bits until the total number of bits is more than or equal to 512.
- **Initialise MD Buffer:** A total of four 32-bit buffers are employed, and the whole string is divided into many blocks of 512 bits each. Set the four buffers to A, B, C, and D.
- **Process Each Block:** Utilizing each sub-block, buffer, and constant array value, four rounds of operations are performed. There are sixteen 32-bit sub-blocks for every 512-bit pool. The final block contains the output message digest. Figure 1.14 shows the MD5 structure.

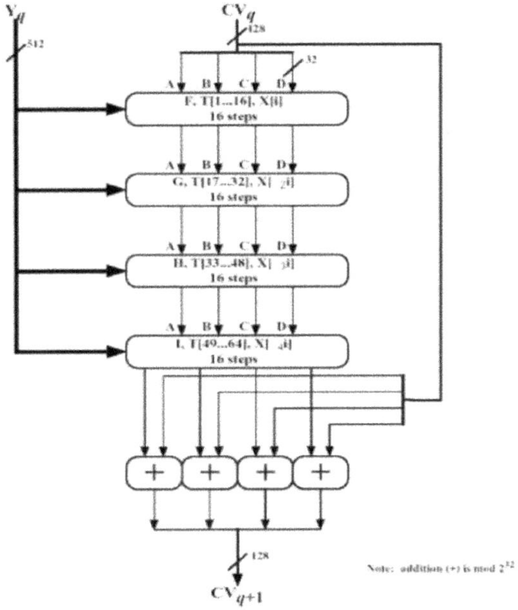

Figure 1.14: MD5 structure

Table 1.1: Comparison Table of all the above Algorithms

Algorithm	Structure	Key Size	Block Size	Rounds	Flexible	Scalability	Processing Speed	Features
DES	Feistel	64 bits	64 bits	16	No	Scalable	Very Low	Not Strong Enough
AES	Substitution Permutation	128, 192, 256 bits	128 bits	10, 12, 14	Yes	Not Scalable	Faster	Security is Excellent, a Replacement for DES
ECC	Public Key Algorithm	More than symmetric var.	Variable	1	Yes	Scalable	Very Fast	Highly Secureand Fast Speed
RSA	Public Key Algorithm	1024 to 4096	128 bits	1	No	Not Scalable	Average	Good Security, Low Speed
Blowfish	Feistel	32–448 bits	64 bits	16	Yes	Scalable	Very Fast	Excellent Security
MD5	Merkle-Damgard Construction	Series of MD	512	4	Yes	Scalable	Fast	Excellent Security

Key structural and performance metrics are used to compare and contrast popular cryptographic algorithms in Table 1.1. A symmetric technique that has been around for a while, DES uses a 64-bit key and block size but isn't flexible and has very slow processing speed, thus it's not a good fit for current applications. AES, which use a substitution-permutation structure and supports key sizes of 128, 192, and 256 bits, delivers excellent security and faster processing but is not inherently scalable across distributed environments. ECC and RSA are both public key algorithms; ECC is perfect for contemporary decentralised and mobile apps since it offers more security with fewer key sizes and is very scalable and quick. RSA, while secure, requires larger key sizes (1024–4096 bits), suffers from slower speed, and lacks scalability. Blowfish, another Feistel structure-based algorithm, supports variable key sizes from 32 to 448 bits, offering very fast and secure encryption, and is scalable for various applications. MD5, based on Merkle-Damgard construction, though once popular for its fast-hashing capabilities, is now considered less secure for cryptographic integrity due to vulnerabilities, despite its scalability and speed. While AES is still a solid choice for symmetric encryption, ECC and Blowfish stand out as promising alternatives for applications that value speed and security equally.

1.8 Self-Signed Key Mechanisms for Robust Protection

1.8.1 Introduction to Key Management Systems

Secure digital communication relies on cryptographic key management systems. Modern digital ecosystems rely heavily on well-managed cryptographic keys to guarantee data privacy, authenticity, and integrity. Traditionally, Public Key Infrastructures (PKI) have served this purpose, with CAs acting as trusted third parties to authenticate digital identities and issue certificates binding public keys to verified identities[59].

While the PKI model has been pivotal in establishing trust over the internet, especially in protocols like HTTPS, it is inherently centralised and fraught with limitations:

- **Single Point of Failure:** An whole certificate chain's trust may be revoked by a hacked CA.

- **Trust Bottlenecks:** Dependence on hierarchical trust models introduces complexity and administrative overhead.
- **Revocation Issues:** Managing certificate revocation remains a persistent problem.
- **Cost:** Commercial certificate issuance incurs significant financial costs[60].

As decentralised technologies like blockchain emerge, there is a pressing need to reimagine key management systems that are autonomous, resilient, and scalable. One such alternative is self-signed keys, which eliminate the need for third-party validation.

1.8.2 Understanding Self-Signed Keys

A digital certificate that bears the signature of the organisation it confirms is known as a self-signed key. Unlike certificates issued by trusted CAs, self-signed certificates do not rely on hierarchical trust but instead promote peer-driven or consensus-based validation mechanisms[61].

1.8.2.1 Components of a Self-Signed Certificate:

- **Public Key:** The cryptographic PublicKey associated with the user or entity.
- **Subject Information:** Metadata identifying the certificate owner (e.g., common name, organization).
- **Issuer Information:** In this case, identical to the subject (self-issued).
- **Validity Period:** The beginning and ending times of the certification.
- **Digital Signature:** Created employing the corresponding private key[62].

1.8.3 Architecture and Working Principles

The architecture of a self-signed key mechanism is characterised by independence and minimal external dependencies. The general operational flow includes:

1. Key Pair Generation

An algorithm such as RSA, ECC, or one of its post-quantum variations (e.g., Falcon, Dilithium) is used to create a cryptographic key pair by the user or device.

2. Certificate Creation and Self-Signing

A certificate is generated containing identity information and the PublicKey, which is then signed using the corresponding PrivateKey [63].

3. Certificate Distribution

The self-signed certificate is shared with other entities, possibly via a peer-to-peer network, blockchain ledger, or decentralised identity registry[64].

4. Verification and Trust Establishment

Since the certificate is not CA-signed, trust is established through mechanisms such as:

- Blockchain consensus
- Web-of-Trust models
- Reputation-based scoring
- Smart contracts enforcing cryptographic proof of origin

This architecture is inherently compatible with distributed systems, allowing seamless integration into blockchain environments and decentralised identity protocols[65].

1.8.4 Integration with Blockchain Systems

The convergence of self-signed certificates and blockchain technology fosters a robust, tamper-resistant, and fully decentralised public key infrastructure (DPKI). Instead than relying on a single CA, confidence in these systems is based on a consensus-driven distributed ledger[66].

1.8.4.1 Key Integration Concepts:

- **Public Key Registration on Blockchain:** Self-signed certificates or their cryptographic digests are placed permanently in the blockchain; this makes them immutable and globally accessible.
- **Smart Contract Verification:** The validation of trust can be automated by using blockchain smart contracts to check certificate details, timestamp, and expiration policies.

- **On-chain Revocation Mechanisms:** Revocation taking place through decentralised revocation lists (CRLs) or Real time revocation through smart contracts enables retired keys based on compromised keys in time.
- **Distributed Key Lookup:** Blockchain acts as a decentralised key directory that applications can query securely[67].

1.8.5 Use Cases of Self-Signed Keys

Another reason self-signed keys are gaining traction is their ability to enable decentralised authentication and data validity independent of centralised Certificate Authorities (CAs). In resource-constrained device authentication in IoT, devices can be independent to generate and register self-signed keys on the blockchain. This guarantees safe on boarding and two-way authentications without third parties[68]. Over in the SSL/TLS context of the decentralised web, blockchain DNS and reputation systems can be used to validate self-signed SSL certificates, enabling websites to remain secure while communicating without the intermediary of the traditional CAs. Another application on the rise is Decentralised Identity (DID), in which users generate self-signed keys and store them on-chain under a self-sovereign identity. This makes it possible to issue verifiable credentials, and it enables users to selectively reveal identity attributes[69]. Moreover, developers should be able to sign their code and binaries using self-signed keys to guarantee the integrity of the software packages. These hashes are posted to a blockchain, which allows authenticity to be verified and the software supply chain to be guarded against tampering and unauthorized modifications.

1.8.6 Technical and Security Considerations

Self-signed keys enable autonomy and decentralisation, but significant risks to security and technology are involved to the use of this method. The first problem is the trust in the establishment without CA. In a decentralized configuration, there must exist distinct methods to authenticate the legitimacy of the self-signed certificates, which are not supplied through a centralized trust authority[70]. MitM attacks represent one of the hazardous risks as malicious users can spread false self-signed keys. The integrity of communication can be undermined by allowing for deception of the recipients where genuine verification methods are wanting.

The other difficulty is with key rotation and lifecycle which entails the integration of mechanisms of key revocation, renewal and expiry without a centralised authority. In the absence of these mechanisms, invalid keys can be accepted as valid, and this is a long-term security threat. Scalability in distribution of keys is also an issue in performance that exists in large-scale decentralised systems. The strategies to distribute and verify the certificates in the network without causing bottlenecks are needed[71]. It is imperative to tackle such concerns in order to realize the maximum benefits of self-signed key mechanisms without compromising security and productivity.

1.9 Motivation

The exponential expansion of online transactions and cloud services has made data security a huge issue for individuals, companies, and governments. Conventional centralized security systems that depend mostly on third-party certificate authorities as well as on unchanging encryption mechanisms are now getting prone to attacks, data leaks, and system crashes. The successive rise in cyber threats like data manipulation, identity impersonation, and unauthorized intrusion has strengthened the necessity of decentralised and unalterable security products. The research is motivated by the potential of Blockchain Technology and self-generated cryptographic keys to create a reliable, scalable, and secure method for protecting digital data. This overall solution to decentralized authentication, removing third-party reliance, and the integrity of the data can be seen as a good avenue towards building trust and resilience in new-fangled online environments.

1.10 Problem Statement

The importance of robust cybersecurity cannot be overestimated in the contemporary digital era with the skyrocket of data-driven services, online transactions, and cloud computing. As organizations, companies, and the services provider shift towards going digital, institutions are becoming vulnerable to sophisticated cyber-attacks on confidentiality, integrity, and availability of sensitive data. Other drawbacks like lack of interoperability across platforms, poor scalability, and single points of failure are limiting traditional centralised security architectures, which rely on trusted third parties like CAs to authenticate and manage keys. Also, maintaining an up-to-date regulatory environment and a smooth passage across multiple digital environments continue to be an issue. Potential outcomes of exploiting such systemic flaws include data breaches, unauthorised access and system disruptions. The intricacy and prevalence of highly hygienic contemporary digital infrastructures demand a solution to information security in a trans figurative method- one that is not centralized, impervious to tampering, and has a potential in facilitating secure communication between different stakeholders. Consequently, it is necessary to consider elaborating upon a secure data protection platform utilizing self-signed crypto keys and blockchain technology. Instead of overcoming the shortcomings of current models, such a system would create a scalable, compliant and interoperable platform to secure digital transactions and enact trust in the cloud-based context.

1.11 Research Question

The following questions must be addressed in this work:

- **RQ1:** Does the use of hybrid encryption and blockchain techniques enhance the confidentiality and integrity of sensitive data in financial and healthcare domains?
- **RQ2:** Can the integration of self-signed cryptographic keys with blockchain technology improve key management and prevent unauthorized access to digital records?
- **RQ3:** How effective is the proposed blockchain-based framework in addressing scalability challenges when managing a large volume of encrypted transactions across financial and healthcare systems?
- **RQ4:** What is the impact of implementing hybrid cryptographic methods on the performance metrics like encryption time, decryption time, memory usage, and throughput in real-time secure data exchange?
- **RQ5:** What technical or operational limitations might arise when deploying a dual-domain blockchain framework combining encryption techniques for securing financial and healthcare records?

1.12 Project aim and objective

Aim

This project aims to improve data confidentiality, integrity, and authenticity by designing and implementing a secure and reliable digital data protection framework. The framework integrates Blockchain technology with cryptographic techniques to address the limitations of centralized security models, ensuring robust and tamper-proof digital record protection for domains such as financial transactions and healthcare systems.

Objectives

- To design a secure system for protecting digital information using Blockchain technology combined with cryptographic techniques.
- To lessen the possibility of unauthorised access and data tampering by using a transparent and immutable Blockchain architecture.
- To implement end-to-end encryption and digital signing using advanced cryptographic algorithms, ensuring secure key management and authentication.
- To identify vulnerabilities in traditional centralized systems and overcome them by adopting a decentralized and verifiable security structure.
- To evaluate the proposed system in relation to more conventional security models; performance, scalability, and efficiency will be evaluated using metrics such as memory utilisation, throughput, and encryption and decryption times.
- To compare the proposed security system to current data security frameworks and technologies in order to determine its performance and resilience.

1.13 Scope of the Research

This study deals with the design and testing of secure digital data protection system combining self-generated cryptographic key methods and blockchain technology. The intended scope encompasses efficient encryption and key management systems, the use of Blockchain Technology to verify information in an immutable scheme. The research focuses on cloud computing and online financial platforms where data integrity, authenticity, and confidentiality play an important role. In addition to deploying a decentralised solution and evaluating the present, susceptible centralised security methods, it will also compare the efficiency, scalability, and security attack resistance of the suggested system to those of existing technologies. The study is restricted to computer-type simulations and assessments, not considering hardware cryptographic implementations, or the regulatory compliance infrastructures other than conceptually.

1.14 Organisation of the Thesis

The following thesis is organized as chapter six:

- **Chapter 2: Literature Review**

  This chapter reviews existing studies on cryptographic encryption algorithms applied in the financial and healthcare domains, with a focus on the integration of Blockchain Technology. The review highlights their strengths and limitations in data protection, authentication, and performance. The chapter also identifies research gaps.

- **Chapter 3: Research Methodology**

  This chapter presents the research framework involving encryption-based security models tailored separately for financial transaction records and healthcare data. The methodology involves designing two secure systems—one for digital financial records and the other for healthcare records—using advanced encryption techniques with blockchain's security.

- **Chapter 4: Implementation Analysis**

  This chapter outlines the hardware and software, and necessary libraries for encryption and blockchain operations. It details the implementation processes for both financial and healthcare records. The chapter analyses data encryption and decryption performance, memory usage, and security validation using simulation results to verify confidentiality and data integrity.

- **Chapter 5: Results and Evaluation**

  The experimental findings, including encryption/decryption time, throughput, and system efficiency for both domains, are presented in this chapter. It talks about the benefits of the suggested dual-domain secure system and compares it to conventional methods. Also, chapter includes research question answers.

- **Chapter 6: Conclusion and Future Work**

  This last chapter provides a concise overview of the study's results and emphasizes its main contributions. It outlines limitations and future work section suggests improvements like integrating federated learning, lightweight consensus mechanisms, advanced key management tools, and expanding the system to edge and IoT environments.

CHAPTER - 2
LITERATURE REVIEW

CONTENTS

Research publications

Advancements in Blockchain Cryptography: Self-Signed Key Applications for Digital Record Protection

Maheshwari, P., Gupta, S., (2025). "Advancements in Blockchain Cryptography: Self-Signed Key Applications for Digital Record Protection", Journal of Applied Engineering and Technological Science, Volume: 6, Issue: 2, pp: 1215 – 1236. DOI: 10.37385/jaets.v6i2.6335

A Novel Decentralized Cryptographic Approach for Robust Authentication of Financial Digital Records Using Blockchain

Maheshwari, P., Gupta, S., (2025). "A Novel Decentralized Cryptographic Approach for Robust Authentication of Financial Digital Records Using Blockchain". Journal of Information Systems Engineering and Management, Volume: 10, Issue: 33. DOI: 10.52783/jisem.v10i33s.5572

2.1 Background

As digital online identities become more integral to many parts of their lives, from personal transactions to employment, healthcare, education, and professional events, digital identity management systems that can easily manage and maintain people's digital identities are becoming more important. It is now an essential part of digital identity management and authentication. Improving data security and system efficiency while decreasing expenses and repetitive procedures is the goal of an advanced IDMS[72].This accelerated the application of cloud networks for storing and making information available [73]. However, traditional implementations of EHRs pose serious issues, including centralised environments, point-to-point hospital communications, and single-point failure [74]. Additionally, keeping private medical information in IoT-based health settings exposes the systems to larger attack surfaces, lowering security and leaving them vulnerable to serious threats like ransomware and DDoS[75].

The integrity of digital records, particularly in the medical sector, is compromised by the implementation of centralised certificate authorities. The dependence of conventional systems on a weak spot puts sensitive data at risk of breaches and unauthorised access. Ensuring the authenticity and integrity of digital data without compromising patient confidentiality is of the utmost importance due to the serious ramifications that might result from any loss. In order to avert such risks, the demand for strong decentralized cryptographic processes that provide security and facilitate the signing and authentication of transactions is growing increasingly[76].

The creation of trust for distributed systems has been radically altered by blockchain technology, which was first developed for the 2008 virtual currency system[77]. Blockchain, with the application of network-wide authentication and consensus of the participating parties, offers secure transactions among the participating parties with no intermediaries [78]which is a revolution for the Internet and IoT transactions [79]. The data structure of a blockchain is the basis for blockchain technology's data authentication and storage capabilities. Consensus algorithms help with data production and updates, while encryption techniques ensure the safe transmission of information[80].

2.2 Related Work

Several researches have tried to implement data security and integrity both when the data is in use and while it is at rest using a variety of techniques, like blockchain technology and homomorphic encryption. The following related work provides in terms of backchain based cryptographic frameworks for digital record security, identity management and authentication using blockchain, lightweight and resource-efficient encryption for IoT and healthcare, and specialized applications of blockchain cryptography.

2.2.1 Blockchain-Based Cryptographic Frameworks for Digital Record Security

2.2.1.1 Blockchain-Based Cryptographic Frameworks for Secure Data Management

In this research, Maheshwari and Gupta (2025) addressed these problems by looking at new developments in blockchain cryptography, particularly the use of self-signed keys for safe digital record keeping. The research recommends a distributed and efficient approach to digital document authentication and maintenance by integrating ECC with a blockchain system. A throughput of 0.0018 tps, an average latency of 3.1790 s for 1000 transactions, and an execution time of 1626.03 s are all metrics that show how efficient the system is according to the experimental assessment of the suggested solution. In comparison to the conventional blockchain implementation, the suggested method guarantees data integrity while reducing encryption and decryption times to 3,650 and 3,968 ms, respectively. Results show that self-signed keys have promise for improving healthcare data security in terms of privacy, authenticity, and integrity[76].

In this study, Ahmad et al. (2023) examined how blockchain, an open ledger system that has attracted attention due to its disruptive power in various industries, uses cryptography. The paper dives into the underlying principles of cryptography, like public key cryptography, Digital Signatures, hashing, and encryptions, and how such theories could be applied to blockchains. Examining cryptography's ability to safeguard user information, preserve data, and call out transactions, this research paper will analyse the blockchain system's reliance on cryptography. Data may be encrypted in a manner that only approved users can decrypt using cryptography, which prohibits unauthorised usage. By generating a new hash value for updated data, hash algorithms ensure data integrity. Digital signatures and public-key encryption combine to make sure that only authorised parties may complete transactions. The article delves into blockchain's cryptographic flaws as well, discussing how public-key cryptography is vulnerable to quantum assaults that might compromise blockchain security. Lastly, the paper focuses on the necessity to maintain blockchain systems safe and resilient when considering future research opportunities and potentials to revolutionise cryptography technology [81].

In this research, Singh and Jain (2023) tested the performance and security of 3 widely utilized encryption algorithms on storage devices that use blockchain technology: RC6, AES, and DES. They demonstrate in their study that each algorithm has both positive and negative sides. The study indicates that numerous various businesses can potentially benefit by enhancing data privacy through blockchain technology combined with cryptographic procedures. Three factors that organisations must consider carefully before adopting such a system are scalability, performance and compliance with regulations. The possible advantages of incorporating cryptographic algorithms into a permission Blockchain System should not be ignored in light of these difficulties. The findings of the study are useful to companies that aim to develop a blockchain that is user-friendly in terms of privacy and security. Performance analysis that considers factors such as RAM, GPU, and CPU utilisation has resulted in findings used to measure the effectiveness of specific algorithms on their model. Security analysis involves key sensitivity and the avalanche effect [82].

2.2.1.2 Privacy-Preserving Blockchain Protocols and Secure Transactions

In this study, Zhang, Li and Fang (2025) proposed the PBTMS which is a blockchain-based privacy protection framework and exploits notions of hybrid encryption, Pedersen commitments, and zero-knowledge proofs to afford high-grade privacy to user data and transaction data. The PBTMS relies on consensus mechanisms and blockchain technology to deliver distributed storage to enable efficient, credible, and safe online purchases by minimizing reliance on potential failures and malicious nodes. The efficient and flexible structure of the PBTMS has been established to take advantage of the dynamic needs of privacy-preserving e-commerce platforms. Theoretical and practical tests indicate that PBTMS significantly outperforms state-of-the-art approaches with a 52.6 percent reduction in authentication and decryption times, a 79.2 percent reduction in encrypted data size, and a 55.4 percent overall gas consumption cut. The findings show that PBTMS is dependable and effective in offering safe e-commerce transaction metropolises and offers a fresh strategy for improving e-commerce privacy protection[83].

In this study Zhang et al. (2024) demonstrated a method for securing data transfers via the use of smart contracts and zero-knowledge solutions. The preparation phase of security parameters is intended to make it easier to produce non-interactive zero-knowledge proofs and to enable more effective data trading. Their development of attribute atomic matching smart contracts paves the way for the supply of fine-grained data property matching among trading partners, provided that data properties are well aligned. The trade execution phase uses two small cryptographic algorithms to encrypt trading data, one using ECC and the other using non-interactive zero-knowledge proofs. Additionally, these algorithms produce contracts that are resistant to attributes, which further protects the material from unlawful access. Research conducted on the Ethereum network inside an industrial IoT environment has shown that their approach ensures a match, anonymity, and consistently low usage [84].

In this research Rangappa et al. (2024) improved data safety and efficiency during cloud migration and storage by using a novel approach that integrates sharding, encryption, ZKPs, and blockchain technologies for controlled access to data and secure database retrieval. Additionally, before saving the content in the cloud, they encrypt it using keys kept in digital wallets that are distinct to each user. These big files (50 MB or larger) or huge data files (greater than 1 TB) exploit the concept of sharding to complicate the use of cloud storage, as they necessitate greater computation. Consequently, the shards of the huge files are stored in various database servers. An additional safeguard that may be used to enhance secure file retrieval and ensure user anonymity is the utilisation of a blockchain smart contract. To guarantee the secure transport of data across various cloud providers, the zk-snark protocol is used. This method ensures data privacy by transmitting just the data's authenticity evidence to the intended cloud validator, rather than the data itself. The presented methodology will ensure compliance with all necessary cloud storage rules, solving crucial difficulties with data security and privacy and efficient resource use in cloud computing environments. Based on the fact that the surrounding promises to protect data privacy of users, and to nowhere store raw data, it can be referred to as a zero-trust paradigm [85].

2.2.1.3 Zero-Trust and Access Control Architectures in Blockchain Systems

In this research, Nie et al. (2025) designed a system for product-level zero-trust access control using Blockchain Technology. In addition, the architecture ensures data security and efficiency via the implementation of smart contract-based automatic access control, inner-product encryption-based fine-grained access control, and a reputation-based trust model–based decentralised identity management system. The first steps include creating software-defined boundaries for various application domains and automating the restriction of smart contract access. Finally, empirical evidence indicates that the method employed in this study yields a massive throughput improvement, a data access latency reduction of 18%, and 14 percent better encryption efficiency compared to the common techniques. System performance and data security are both well-managed by this approach in scenarios involving many data connections [86].

In this research, Lin (2023) proposed blockchain architecture similar to multi-tier to secure data of the Internet of automobiles. A block, inside-cluster, and inter-cluster blockchain are all components of the proposed multi-tiered blockchain architecture. The roadside unit (RSU) manages transmissions over the Internet of vehicles to enable information exchange amongst neighbouring cars. The study uses RSU for block management, and the Base Station oversees the intra-cluster blockchain, which is referred to as intra-cluster BC. The system's blockchain, including cluster BC, is overseen by the remote Cloud Server. Collaboration between RSUs, Base Station, and Cloud Server forms a multi-tiered blockchain architecture that enhances the security and efficiency of blockchain operations. Their main objectives in suggesting a novel structure for transaction blocks and using the ECDSA to secure blockchain transaction data are to guarantee the authenticity of the Merkle tree root value and to provide non-repudiation of transaction data. Last but not least, this research takes cloud computing security into account; as a result, they suggest an architecture that uses the identity confirmation technique to reduce secure maps and facilitate secret sharing [87].

2.2.1.4 Advanced and Post-Quantum Cryptographic Methods for Blockchain Security

In this study, Raj, Kurt Peker and Mutlu (2024) proposed a blockchain solution that secures the data and guarantees statistical privacy in its share with other parties to study or analyze by deploying fully homomorphic encryption.The proposed system can protect data during transmission, storage, processing, ensure confidentiality and accuracy of basic statistical calculations. A proposed system performs statistical calculations on Data encrypted, including mean, median, and variance, and is deployed to the Zama blockchain. The findings prove that the blockchain can handle completely homomorphic computations. The suggested system would provide a thorough solution to the application security issue, taking into account concerns about confidentiality, integrity at rest, in transit, and during usage, as well as data and statistics privacy. However, the system would not be able to handle large data sets at the moment because of limitations in blockchain computing. Further improvements in homomorphic operations on blockchains will further enable this system to function[88].

In this research, Lahraoui et al. (2024) established a new hashing-based algorithm of encrypting messages that can be embedded into the EC points. The approach is made more secure by using a shared secret point and a randomly generated parameter from the EC Diffie-Hellman protocol. The inputs, complexity, and sensitivity of the encryption system are also examined, and the suggested technique's security is evaluated in relation to a number of potential assaults. The NIST statistical test suite was applied to ascertain whether the ciphertext was random. To further guarantee the message's integrity, they are also suggesting a method of securely attaching a tag to the cipher text. Therefore, their proposal is effective in guarding data against most forms of attacks based on a comprehensive analysis. Besides being workable, linearly complex, and satisfying the strict avalanche condition, the method also satisfies other conditions[89].

In this research, Long et al. (2023) investigated the cryptography-based security issues with blockchains, like Cryptographic Homomorphic Encryption, ZKP, and secure multi-party computing. Public Key Cryptography based on hashes, Public Key Cryptography based on codes, multivariate Public Key Cryptography, and lattice-based PublicKey Cryptography are the four most viable post-quantum cryptography approaches examined in this paper. Current cryptography systems, and blockchains in particular, are likely to be affected by the advancement of quantum computing[90].

2.2.1.5 Application-Specific Blockchain Security Solutions

In this study, Guediri et al. (2025) showcased an HMPS method developed to tackle the difficulties of distributed and limited resource systems. In HMPS, increased security is offered through collaborative and layered signing protocols, linear encryption, and a variant ElGamal-based individual signature. Comparisons to state-of-the-art algorithms demonstrate that HMPS is computationally more efficient, better scalable, and energy consuming. The results indicate that HMPS is an excellent strategy to enhance reliability and security of distributed systems and that it well suits real-time IoT applications [91].

In this research, Habibi Markani et al. (2023) sought to improve ADS-B security by exposing the shortcomings of existing systems and evaluating the practicability of using FormatPreserving (F), Feistel-based Encryption (F), with various Implementation Variants (X) (FFX) methods. An industry-standard SDR ADS-B is used to implement the provided solution for real-time applications. In addition, the cypher key is managed using a newly developed blockchain technique, which functions as a secure database. An algorithm's capacity to muddle and disperse predictable ADS-B signals may be evaluated using the message entropy measure. One way to measure the safety of the suggested approach is to compare the plain and cypher data using correlation and serial correlation. The authors prove the approach's viability using flying test results and MATLAB simulations. Their technique may be able to safeguard ADS-B information privacy, according to their security study. The performance assessment findings show that the suggested method can be used in the avionics industry[92].

In thier research, Fouzar, Lakhssassi and Mundugar (2023) improved the safety of video footage by using a multi-key method for encryption and decryption. The goal indicated earlier was achieved by combining several approaches, creating dynamic keys, and using procedures based on user attributes. Improving the safety protocols linked to the creation of video content was the major aim of the research. An integral aspect of using the proposed approach is the use of a pseudorandom key in conjunction with a series of mathematical formulae. The encryption method's level of security is significantly enhanced by this unique methodology. A proposed method uses randomised combination of mathematical equations to achieve encryption. Random selection will enhance overall security of the system. The suggested strategy involves dividing the movie into portions, known as chunks. Subsequently, the individual sections are coded with separate keys, which are created on the fly in real time. The Android platform is used to execute the suggested procedure. The user views the video through the receiver application, and the transmitter application is responsible to facilitate the live and streaming of content. The suggested strategy was compared to other comparable tactics that had been utilised before in thorough research. The results of the study offer substantial confirmation that the provided treatment is safe and reliable[93].

Badr, Zhang and Ahmad Umar (2019) proposed a novel approach to facilitate an attribute-based encryption system (ABE) that incorporates a number of stakeholders, including cloud servers, authorities, data owners, and users. The essential component of their suggested design is a validated and certified decryption procedure for the cloud environment. Data encryption is a pre-processing step before data is sent to the cloud. The data is encrypted in part by the cloud server, and only authorised users may access the final, decrypted version. The data owner may simplify and expedite the decryption process by leaving it to the cloud server. The findings of the experiment show that a managed multiple-user rights framework makes data access in the electronic cloud environment safer. They found that the suggested architecture improves DICOM security while decreasing communication overhead in their performance evaluations.

Digital record security using blockchain-based cryptographic frameworks is summarised in Table 2.1[94].

Table 2.1: Summary of Related Works on Blockchain-Based Cryptographic Frameworks for Digital Record Security

Author(s), Year	Proposed Method/System	Technologies Used	Application Domain	Key Outcomes
Maheshwari & Gupta, 2025	Blockchain with self-signed keys using ECC	Blockchain, ECC, Self-signed keys	Digital health records	Achieved 0.0018 tps throughput, latency 3.1790 s; improved confidentiality and security with low encryption time.
Zhang, Li & Fang, 2025	PBTMS privacy-preserving blockchain framework	Hybrid encryption, Pedersen commitments, ZKPs	E-commerce	79.2% data size reduction, 52.6% faster decryption; secure and low-overhead transaction protection.
Nie et al., 2025	Zero-trust access control architecture	Smart contracts, Inner-product encryption, Multi-chain blockchain	6G IoT systems	18% latency reduction; enhanced trust and access management in dense data environments.
Guediri et al., 2025	HMPS multi-layered signing protocol	ElGamal, Layered encryption, Collaborative signatures	IoT / Vehicle surveillance	Improved scalability, energy-efficiency, and real-time data integrity.
Raj, Peker & Mutlu,	Blockchain + Fully	FHE, Smart contracts, Zama	Statistical data	Enables encrypted mean/median/varianc

2024	Homomorphic Encryption	blockchain	privacy	e on-chain; limited by large data sizes.
Zhang et al., 2024	Secure data trading with ZKPs & ECC	Attribute-matching smart contracts, non-interactive ZKPs, ECC	Industrial IoT	Ensures anonymous, efficient and attribute-aligned secure trading.
Rangappa et al., 2024	Secure cloud storage with sharding & zk-SNARK	Sharding, ZKPs, Blockchain, Digital wallets	Cloud migration	Guarantees privacy, regulatory compliance; zero-trust paradigm for cloud.
Lahraoui et al., 2024	EC-based hash embedding encryption	ECC, Diffie-Hellman, NIST test suite	Secure messaging	Meets avalanche criteria; secure against attacks; ensures ciphertext randomness.
Lin, 2023	Multi-tier blockchain for Internet of Vehicles	ECDSA, Merkle tree, RSUs, Inter/Intra cluster blockchains	Internet of Vehicles	Improved authenticity and decentralised coordination of vehicular data.
Long et al., 2023	Post-quantum blockchain cryptographic review	Homomorphic encryption, ZKP, MPC, Hash/code/lattice-based crypto	General blockchain security	Explores quantum-resistant alternatives for blockchain systems.
Ahmad et al., 2023	Blockchain cryptography fundamentals	Digital Signatures, Hashing, Public key encryption	General blockchain architecture	Discusses blockchain's dependency on cryptography and its vulnerability to quantum threats.
Singh & Jain, 2023	Performance testing of RC6, AES, and DES in blockchain	RC6, AES, DES encryption algorithms	Storage systems with blockchain	Highlights performance trade-offs; emphasises scalability and compliance.
Habibi Markani et al., 2023	ADS-B privacy via Feistel-based Format Preserving Encryption (FFX)	SDR, FFX, Blockchain-based key management, MATLAB	Aviation / ADS-B systems	Proven privacy enhancement through live testing; suitable for avionics.

Fouzar, Lakhssassi & Mundugar, 2023	Multi-key encrypted video streaming	Android, Dynamic keys, Random equations, Chunking	Encrypted multimedia streaming	High security in live video transmission; real-time key generation.
Badr, Zhang & Umar, 2019	Attribute-based Encryption (ABE) for cloud	ABE, Certified decryption, Multi-user access management	Cloud storage / DICOM	Efficient decryption; reduced communication overhead; secure multi-user data access.

2.2.2 Identity Management and Authentication Using Blockchain

2.2.2.1 Decentralized Identity Management Systems (IDMS) and Smart Contracts

In this research,Alanzi and Alkhatib (2025) recommended major objective of IDMS is to guarantee the privacy and secrecy of users' individual data. For user data storage and authentication, traditional IDMS employ a third-party service. This strategy, however, raises the possibility of SPOF, User Tracking, and Data Unavailability in addition to endangering user privacy. On the other hand, decentralised IDMSs that make employ of BlockchainTechnology provide viable answers to these problems by offering potent characteristics like decentralisation, anonymity, transparency, and immutability. Although it has many advantages, blockchain technology is not without drawbacks and poor authentication, performance problems, third party control, and data leakage have been among its issues. Moreover, centralisation issues in some blockchain-based IDMSs may also compromise the privacy of the users and the risk of SPOF. The problems with centralised IDMSs are addressed in this paper by proposing a distributed IDMS that uses blockchain and smart contracts. A suggested system is equally enhanced by utilising the IPFS to reduce the load on-chain storage can carry. Furthermore, the ECIES is used by the proposed IDMS to enhance system transaction efficiency, safeguard users' private data, and provide an additional layer of safety. Comparing the suggested IDMS to its competitors, security analysis and testing findings showed that it provides significant security and performance benefits[95].

Siyal et al. (2024) studied an MPA system that runs on blockchain to securely store and access data, provide reliable audit trails, and employs different authorities to enable authentication and authorisation. The research improves a hybrid key-generation method that uses the IABHE Algorithm and DSNN, or IABHE+DSNN, to facilitate safe data transmission to a blockchain-based system that involves several parties. This strategy achieves data security by incorporating many security abilities and various organisations. Authentication on all fronts, initial registration, data security, validation, and exchange are all part of the iterative process. To secure data, the MapReduce architecture use DSNN to generate keys and IABHE to oversee encryption. An experimental result shows that the suggested IABHE+DSNN method outperforms the advance methods according to decryption time (10.786), encryption time (15.765), and key complexity (0.887)[96].

Shi, Zeng and Han (2022) invented a new model of distributed authentication, which supports public key cryptography using a secure mechanism. Their method leverages the DID project to build a decentralised PublicKey infrastructure by combining blockchain smart contracts with efficient zero-knowledge proof-verifiable presentations. This approach ensures that public keys within a decentralised infrastructure are available and valid because they can be managed through blockchain. Their scheme is more scalable in authenticating data source and addresses security and practicability issues encountered in earlier methodologies. Experimental data indicate that their concept outperforms the original zero-knowledge proof technique in registration by 20% [97].

2.2.2.2 Blockchain-Based PKI for Secure Authentication

Haindl (2024) studied potential applications of the blockchain-based PKI and compared it to the traditional PKI products. Finding out if a decentralised PKI can make use of BlockchainTechnology requires weighing the pros and cons of the two methods. The research will also evaluate the current legislative tools such as the NIS-2 Directive and the CRA. The study will review different blockchain PKI implementations based on the factors such as platform, security, and performance. The outcomes show that blockchain-based PKIs can be more secure than conventional PKIs and so address its limitations due to the decentralisation of the trust anchor. Blockchain technology ensures that managing certificates is visible and cannot be reversed, significantly boosting the complexity of attempts to tamper.

There are also superior approaches to detecting and remediating certificate fraud with blockchain-based PKIs [98].

Halder, Das Roy and Shin (2024) they demonstrate the way blockchain technology, a mix of decentralised certificate verification, would respond and neutralise such attacks. To circumvent problems with issued certificates and single points of failure, they provide a decentralised PKI that is based on a distributed trust paradigm, like blockchain technology and the WoT. Along with improved certificate security and revocation, their approach offers a reliable key-ring network that separates authentication from CAs. They also illustrate deployment of their system within the Ethereum blockchain as evidence of concept, establishing that their model fulfils the five conditions. Their proposed approach uses more overhead than standard PKIs; however, the results of their open-source tests indicate that the approach is practical[99].

Javed et al. (2022)enquired about the possibility of a blockchain serving as a CA and a transaction as a certificate. Their goal is to make it easier to utilise a blockchain without relying on CAs or a TTP. In their security research, they show that the suggested method is resilient against both known and new types of attacks. Device impersonation, replay, de-synchronisation, DoS, and MITMattacks are all defeated by the proposed technique. It finds that the suggested system is better in terms of computing and communication costs as well as security features when comparing its performance and security to those of comparable current methods. The suggested method has a total computing cost of 40.479 milliseconds, which is lower than the 37.49% and 49.79% of the two similar techniques. This proves that, compared to competing systems, the suggested one works better in an IoD setting[100].

In this study, Boyen et al. (2021) proposed DPKIT: transparent certificate issuance and revocation with the removal of any failure points using a client-based, decentralised method. The DPKIT system builds an append-only distributed associative array on top of an existing blockchain. Anyone, or their browser, may access and edit the public record of certificate issuance and revocations for any given domain using this array. Their work on these fronts includes a security model for transparent certificates, the definition of append-only associative ledgers, and a formal analysis of their DPKIT architecture. Compared to federated solutions employed by Google or the Electronic Frontier Foundation, a client-side browser plugin like DPKIT would do a significantly better job of detecting and prosecuting fraud very early on with user acceptability due to its range and anonymity. Table 2.2 below summarises relevant studies on blockchain-based identity management and authentication[101].

2.2.2.3 Privacy-Preserving and Regulatory-Compliant Blockchain Authentication

In this study, Peng et al. (2024) proposed how to achieve privacy in blockchain transactions using the latest cryptography in a blockchain coupled with digital mutual trust system. An innovative dynamic Byzantine consensus method that incorporates an authorisation mechanism from the reputation model into the Practical Byzantine Fault Tolerance model is one of the contributions. Strong digital mutual trust may also be achieved by a proof consensus technique. A further optimisation of homomorphic cryptography utilising the approximate greatest common divisor approach is implemented to secure complex activities. Smart contracts enable the confidential and automatic performance of transactions on blockchains. The results of the experiments demonstrate that this approach is much more efficient and accurate than previous ones when handling privacy requests and transaction receipts[102].

In this study, Li et al. (2024) discovered a way to resolve the issue of how to control transactions through the blockchain but maintain the privacy of the user, and they proposed a scheme to execute this. They would like to conceal the true identity of blockchain transaction participants through probabilistic public-key encryption. The DL graph neural network tech combines with the zero-knowledge proof approaches and commitment schemes to protect user privacy and enable regulatory scrutiny of blockchain transaction data. The approach ensures that regulations are adhered to both macro and micro levels, which confirm legitimacy of transactions and also ensures leakage of critical transaction information is avoided. The computational and storage requirements of managing keys would be tremendously lessened as regulatory bodies used an identity-based encryption protocol to personally monitor blockchain transactions, but not retain the actual identities and key information of users. Their proposal collaborates with the current blockchain technology and is not dependent on a particular consensus procedure. It demonstrates the viability of the scheme based on simulation trial and complexity analysis [103].

Table 2.2: Summary of Related Works on Identity Management and Authentication Using Blockchain

Author(s), Year	Proposed System/Model	Techniques Used	Focus Area	Key Contributions/ Outcomes
Alanzi & Alkhatib, 2025	Decentralized IDMS with ECIES & IPFS	Blockchain, Smart Contracts, ECIES, IPFS	User Identity Management	Enhances privacy, decentralization, and performance; reduces on-chain storage issues and SPOF.
Haindl, 2024	Blockchain-based PKI alternatives	Blockchain PKI, NIS-2 Directive, CRA	Certificate Management	More secure than traditional PKI; improved fraud detection and trust transparency.
Siyal et al., 2024	MPA System with IABHE+DSNN	Hybrid Key Gen, DSNN, IABHE, MapReduce, Blockchain	Multi-Party Authentication	10.78s decryption, 15.76s encryption; better key complexity and performance than current systems.
Peng et al., 2024	Privacy-aware Digital Trust System	Homomorphic Encryption, Byzantine Consensus, Smart Contracts	Private Blockchain Transactions	Reduces delays, boosts accuracy in handling privacy requests and receipts.
Halder, Das Roy & Shin, 2024	Decentralised PKI using WoT on Ethereum	Blockchain, WoT (Web of Trust), Ethereum	Certificate Verification	Enhanced certificate security; resists revocation issues and improves decentralisation.
Li et al.,	Probabilistic	DL Graph	Transaction	Hides identities;

Author(s), Year	Proposed System/Model	Techniques Used	Focus Area	Key Contributions/ Outcomes
2024	Public Key Encryption + ZKP	NN, ZKP, Commitment Schemes, Identity-Based Encryption	Privacy and Regulation	supports oversight without compromising user data.
Javed et al., 2022	Blockchain as CA for Authentication	Blockchain Certificates, No TTP, DoS-resilient design	IoD (Internet of Devices) Authentication	40.47 ms compute time; defeats impersonation and replay attacks; superior to existing schemes.
Shi, Zeng & Han, 2022	DID-based PKI with Zero-Knowledge Proofs	DID, Blockchain Smart Contracts, Verifiable Credentials	Distributed Authentication Infrastructure	20% faster registration; scalable, secure, and decentralized.
Boyen et al., 2021	DPKIT – Client-side Certificate Management	Append-only Distributed Ledger, Browser Plugin, Certificate Transparency	PKI, Certificate Issuance/ Revocation	Detects fraud early; more transparent and anonymous than federated models (e.g., Google CT logs).

2.2.3 Lightweight and Resource-Efficient Encryption for IoT and Healthcare

In this research, Belfqih and Abdellaoui (2025) presented a decentralised authentication mechanism in which IPFS data management architecture and blockchain technology offer secure and real-time communication among IoTdevices. The suggested protocol helps to secure sensitive IoT data against unauthorized access, alteration, or deletion through smart contracts, ECC, and the Ethereum blockchain with ASCON encryption. The mutual authentication protocol creates a shared secret using a publicly published key on the blockchain, an asymmetric key pair, and the Diffie Hellman algorithm for key exchange in order to certify the secure device. Also, IPFS is utilized to store data safely; to authenticate and track the data, the CID is inserted into the blockchain and then encrypted with ASCON.

This combined approach serves as the good foundation of next applications in decentralised IoT environments and addresses current IoT security challenges[104].

Sabri et al. (2025) explored low-overhead cryptography solutions that can be used in IoT healthcare applications and evaluated the extent to which they offered protection to sensitive information when operated on small resources. The key features of the encryption algorithms AES-128, LEA, Ascon, GIFT, HIGHT, PRINCE, and RC5-32/12/16 are compared according to valuable criteria as BlockSize, KeySize, the speed of encryption and decryption, the throughput, and security. According to the results, the strongest security measures for highly sensitive healthcare data are AES-128, LEA, ASCON, and GIFT, while the finest safe measures for medium-sensitive applications are PRINCE and HIGHT. Vice versa, RC5-32/12/16 would fit better in a low-risk environment where the CPU overhead must be minimal because it is more focused on efficiency than security. Research shows that there are considerable trade-offs among efficiency, security, and resource consumption, thus it's important to carefully choose encryption algorithms that meet the needs of IoT healthcare systems. It also points out the growing importance of energy-efficient, lightweight cryptography which can withstand online attacks effectively. Researchers and healthcare professionals interested in learning more about how to make IoT-based healthcare systems more secure and how to get the most out of facilities with limited resources would find these insights to be very helpful[105].

Ahmed and Roseth (2025) looked into the interplay between quantum computing and blockchain technology, regarding how quantum resistant cryptographic methods may defend blockchain networks. It talks about the important developments in quantum-secure algorithms, how QKD can secure digital transactions, and what quantum-enabled smart contracts may achieve. The use of quantum technology into pre existing blockchain systems determines a number of issues, including processing prices, compatibility with current systems, and scalability. By combining quantum computing with Blockchain Technology, it can usher in a new age of information security where sensitive data is safe from both novel and ubiquitous cyber attacks[106].

2.2.3.1 Blockchain-Enhanced Privacy and Security in IoT

In this study, Ali et al. (2023) designed a revolutionary PoC framework addressing blockchain-based privacy concerns in CPSs via consortium blockchain technology. The aim of the proposed architecture is to protect confidential information and ensure data integrity without losing the trust of stakeholders. The technology guarantees anonymity with control over a decentralised and immutable framework through consortium blockchain technology. Nonetheless, it faces significant obstacles in guaranteeing the safety and security of private data stored in CPSs. The current work proposes a state-of-the-art privacy approach where the CPS secrets protection is based on consortium Blockchain Technology. Consortium blockchain offers a reliable basis to manage the network and confirm the transactions as it is based on the permissioned model. CPS secrets may be stored, distributed, and made available only to authorised parties by employing consortium Blockchain Technology to reduce its exposure to data breaches and illegal access. The suggested method is beneficial through improved security, privacy preservation, and trust, accountability, interoperability and scalability. This research seeks to enhance CPS security and privacy by using consortium blockchain to revolutionise secret management and addressing the shortcomings of current security procedures. Deep performance evaluations and simulations reflect an effectiveness of a design. Drawing on the outcomes, the proposed approach advances significantly in privacy protection which paves the way to trustworthy cyber-physical systems in numerous industries [107].

Al Hwaitat et al. (2023) solutions built on the blockchain that improve the state of IoT networks are gaining a lot of traction. For the sake of IoT security, a decentralised authentication framework based on the blockchain might be used to securely interact between devices and external systems by storing and verifying their identities. Complexity and storage overhead are the primary problems with the current blockchain-based IoT technology. Their innovative solution to these research problems is a permissions-based blockchain-based huge IoT system that optimises data storage and offers consumers a lightweight authentication method. Most applications built on the blockchain stand to benefit from the proposed method's capacity to optimise storage and increase scalability. They have also pioneered the use of HE to encrypt user-end IoT data before sending it to the cloud. Using comprehensive simulation results, the suggested approach is contrasted with various benchmark frameworks. Their work aids in the development of a new IoT strategy that integrates first-rate IoT services while improving privacy and security via the use of a trust-aware security architecture [108].

In this study, Khan and Byun (2020) proposed a strategy of picture security and encryption based on permissioned private blockchain. To ensure the privacy and security of the image data, one strategy for this project is to record the cryptographic pixel count on the blockchain. They check the strength of the proposed picture encryption algorithms against the differential attack by using quantities such as information entropy examination, unitary average changed intensity (UACI) and NPCR. They were able to achieve entropy levels that are quite close to 8 which is the magic number that resists brute force attacks. Encrypted results indicate when the proposed method is significantly more secure and a data leakage is avoided [109].

In this study, Kim, Kim and Huh (2019) used the newly formed Blockchain Technology to fix the security problems with current IoT devices. There is also the application of this technology for M2M access payment via the KYD method, which depends on the dependability of pre-existing IoT devices. Consequently, this research proposes a BoT ecosystem to address concerns related to logistics management and historical record management, specifically the hacking risk associated with IoT devices. The sensor multi-platform also has several security flaws, which is a problem from an IoT perspective. To solve the problem of security holes in sensor multi-platforms, this study applies blockchain technology to a real-world scenario. In order to improve TPS performance and measure different security strengths using the multiple-agreement technique, this study mentions a colour spectrum chain as a blockchain concept. Finally, to address the issues with automobile, aviation, and CCV sensor equipment, they propose using the core algorithm radix of a blockchain. The fact that all IoT devices depend on wireless technology is a huge drawback when it comes to utilising them over wired networks.

There is more than one way for security to be compromised, and sensors are easy targets for hackers. Their goal remains the same: to show that the colour spectrum chain has robust authentication capabilities and to apply it to sensors and blockchain-based multi-platforms, regardless of how many security gaps there may be in IoT devices. The following table 2.3 provide the summary of related work on Lightweight and Resource-Efficient Encryption for IoT and Healthcare [110].

2.2.3.2 Blockchain for Source Code and Digital Asset Protection

In this study, Ramirez Lopez and Morillo Ledezma (2025) examined digital technologies that strengthen the security of source code, including NFTs and Blockchain. As a result of Blockchain's decentralised and unchangeable nature, NFTs have the potential to regulate code ownership, which would enhance security, traceability, and prohibit unauthorised access. The deficiencies in academic intellectual property protection that now exist are successfully filled by this strategy. Despite the huge potential that such technologies have, Bennett et al. acknowledge the fact that both user adoption and deployment across the board continues to pose a challenge. These challenges offer an opportunity to enhance academic integrity using NFTs or blockchain integration despite this setback. This may require a more creative and embracing strategy to succeed in the educational contexts[111].

2.2.3.3 Blockchain and Federated Learning for Privacy-Preserving IoT

In this study, Wang and Li (2024) to address these barriers, proposed a novel type of cloud-edge orchestrated federated learning with a hierarchical blockchain approach, named HBCE-FL. HBCE-FL can provide distributed, smart, and secure data analysis to IoT consumers. They propose addressing the privacy shortcomings of FL by adopting blockchain to establish an encryption and multi-level access control solution to the HBCE-FL framework of IoT data exchange. Their method divides IoT users into many tiers according to their specific privacy needs, allowing for fine-grained privacy protection. The blockchain is used in message encryption, keys adjustment and identity checks. They supplement HBCE-FL with federated multi-task learning to enhance it in situations where IoT users handle data that lacks IID. Lastly, they confirm their technique via tests conducted on the traditional MNIST and CIFAR10 datasets. The findings of the experiment show that HBCE-FL successfully accomplishes personalised privacy-preserving FL while retaining the availability of IoT data. They enhance the accuracy and convergence rate of models, as they enable users to share and access IoT knowledge securely, whether the data provided by IoT devices are or are not homogeneous[112].

In this research, Sun et al. (2024) proposed a system of privacy-preserving distributed learning, where unfair parties could not access the data, and every participant could share and receive data but not people under suspicion. They use a contribution assessment system on encrypted data to stop free-riding assaults and data poisoning, and they use cryptography-based data privacy mitigation to stop data leaks during blockchain transactions. Moreover, the group employs Shamir secret sharing to bargain a secret key; the bargained key is subsequently presented to the model as a noise ensuring that the encryption operation is computationally economical. By relying on encrypted models across the group, efficient decryption and encryption are both optimized in the computing power required. Finally, their proposed approach is effective and effective, as illustrated by the experiments[113].

2.2.3.4 Blockchain for Secure Data Sharing and Cloud Security

Wu et al. (2024) proposed a new decentralised solution of sharing encrypted financial information, Chain Maker Privacy Computing (CPC) system, to solve this problem. To ensure data privacy, it offers a data structure and a collection of financial data rather than keeping real data on the blockchain. They provide a safe environment where the local database may use smart contracts to decrypt the data. The team develops a resource catalogue that can be visualised on the blockchain so as to offer an ability to portray a trusted environment on the consumption of the privacy computing system data. They come up with a CPC-CP-ABE, a variation of CP-ABE, that allows for granular access control by means of attribute-based encryption. They end with a practical way to allow authorised data-sharing systems to search encrypted text using Boolean logic. All blockchain-based companies may accomplish trustworthy data exchange with the help of the CPC system, as shown in the trial [114].

Yeboah-Ofori, Sadat and Darvishi (2023) explored how encryption mechanisms and Blockchain Technology could improve security of clouds by maintaining the privacy of the user and integrity of information. The present study contributes three novelties to the table. The authors start by having a glimpse of the numerous blockchain threats, flaws, and their impact on the cloud-computing ecosystem. This ecosystem is supported by an array of cloud services which allow users to share and store data online. The combination of AES encryption, cloud storage, and an Ethereum Smart Contract on the AWS S3 Cloud further enhanced data security. Finally, they propose the inclusion of control processes to ensure cloud systems are safeguarded with blockchain. Findings demonstrate that using AES algorithms in blockchain smart contracts ensures data storage and transfer security [115].

Pióro et al. (2024) focused on the challenge of maintaining the data-centric security model, incorporating an implementation of fine-grained access controls and the assurance of secure data transmission between an origin source and its recipients. ABE is one of the innovative methods that can be applied to destroy this problem. Their work defines a detailed blueprint of safe data transfer within a MIoT federation by using Hyperledger Fabric as a distributed registry, Apache Kafka as a message broker, and micro services based on the Kafka Streams API that process the data. After designing and implementing ABE cryptography data access control algorithms that used pairing-based ECC combined with lightweight cryptography, they confirmed its relevance in the context of military network federations. The proposed cryptographic method offers a practical trade-off between security and speed of modern cryptographic schemes as evident by experimental results, and the extent of characteristics is widely deployed in combats networks[116].

In this research, Yang and Tsai (2024) proposed a hot and cold block approach to be the foundation of a blockchain data storage mechanism. A block heat assessment approach can help them establish which blocks receive the heaviest traffic and base the blockchain nodes on historical and correlation-based heat signatures. Conversely, the data blocks with lesser access frequency are commonly referred to as cold blocks, are stored in the cloud. As a result, blockchain nodes will have less data to store. To implement access control mechanisms, improve security, and preserve privacy, encryption is a must in blockchain-based applications like healthcare and government services. They offer a way to store encrypted data on the chain which utilizes threshold secret sharing to address this issue. The numerous segments of the encryption key to blockchain information must be distributed to network nodes through threshold secret sharing technology. These key segments are further encrypted before being stored using public keys. The approach also complicates the effort of attackers to access blockchain data. Moreover, they proposed an encryption technique that keeps the encryption keys associated with the block contents. This method effectively combats weak password attacks. Their approach is demonstrated to be effective in relieving network storage pressure on blockchain nodes, providing economical encryption storage of data[117].

In this study, Liu, Liang and Lyu (2024) introduced a blockchain and privacy-friendly SSI creation system. The method they've developed satisfies the fundamental needs of SSI users for safe, cross-domain identity and data exchange using unique blockchain digital signatures. Their approach has several advantages in practice over existing solutions to SSI. These are lower cost of the implementation, increased user understanding and acceptability, and better chance of societal and legal institutions adoption. The innovative technical features include three main points: (1) an impenetrable system that minimises the possibility of data breaches while keeping data "usable but invisible"; (2) a system for service providers to review each other to avoid abuse and excessive data requests; and (3) a system for comprehensive multi-party supervision that audits everyone involved and eliminates misconduct[118].

2.2.3.5 Blockchain and Quantum-Resistant Security

In this research, Ahmed et al. (2023) proposed a secure cyber security system based on ELCA that address the weak bits problem using a shared secret key and use ECDH for key distribution. Three different integration systems are examined in this study. To make it easier for IoT devices to communicate insecurely while maintaining message secrecy and authenticity, ELCA suggests a safe combination of encryption and authentication. IoT adversary and random oracle models are also used to mathematically demonstrate the security of ELCA. Results from the simulation show that ELCA successfully cuts basic cryptographic techniques' Execution Time by 50%, Storage Cost by 32-19.6%, and energy use by 41%[119].

In this research, Zaidi et al. (2021) offered a concept for Internet of Things access control based on attributes. Not all device's access control lists are necessary for the system to function. From an efficiency standpoint, it improves access management. They also employ blockchain technology to track attributes, prevent data tampering, and eliminate the weak spot in edge computing equipment. IoT devices regulate the user's surroundings and data collecting, which raises the risk of privacy breaches due to the exposure of users' personal information to untrusted servers, whether public or private. The system may be automated and data can be accessed with the use of smart contracts. To maximise efficiency and reduce petrol waste, Proof of Authority is used. The data owner might store cipher text on a blockchain using smart contracts. Blockchains record invocations and create smart contracts to achieve the trace function, however data could only be decrypted within the valid access time. The multichain blockchain has the potential to solve scalability problems. The results of the simulations show that the suggested method works well for IoT systems[120].

Table 2.3: Summary of Related Works on Lightweight and Resource-Efficient Encryption for IoT and Healthcare

Author(s), Year	**Proposed System/Model**	**Techniques Used**	**Focus Area**	**Key Contributions/ Outcomes**
Belfqih & Abdellaoui, 2025	Decentralised IoT Authentication Protocol	IPFS, Blockchain, Smart Contracts, ECC, ASCON, Diffie-Hellman	IoT Authentication & Secure Communication	Combines ASCON encryption with IPFS and ECC to secure real-time IoT communication.
Sabri et al., 2025	Comparative Study of Lightweight Cryptography	AES-128, LEA, ASCON, GIFT, PRINCE, HIGHT, RC5	Lightweight Cryptography for IoT Healthcare	Identifies optimal encryption algorithms for various levels of healthcare data sensitivity.

Ahmed & Roseth, 2025	Quantum-Resistant Cryptographic Integration	Quantum Secure Algorithms, QKD, Smart Contracts	Blockchain-Quantum Cryptography	Introduces quantum-based cryptography for securing blockchain systems.
Ramirez Lopez & Morillo Ledezma, 2025	Blockchain and NFTs for Code Ownership	Blockchain, NFT	Digital IP Protection	Secures code ownership using NFTs to enhance traceability and access control.
Wang & Li, 2024	HBCE-FL Framework	Hierarchical Blockchain, Federated Learning, Access Control	Federated IoT Data Privacy	Improves privacy in federated learning using blockchain-based access controls.
Wu et al., 2024	ChainMakerPrivacyComputing (CPC)	CP-ABE, Smart Contracts, Privacy Computing	Encrypted Financial Data Sharing	Enables granular access and secure financial data sharing via CPC-CP-ABE.
Sun et al., 2024	Privacy-Preserving Distributed Learning	Shamir Secret Sharing, Noise Injection, Cryptographic Privacy	Secure Distributed ML	Defends against data leaks and poisoning in collaborative ML.
Pióro et al., 2024	ABE-based MIoT Security Framework	ABE, ECC, Hyperledger, Kafka	Military IoT Data Security	Implements ECC and ABE to ensure secure federated data transmission.
Yang & Tsai, 2024	Hot-Cold Block Storage Mechanism	Secret Sharing, Public Key Encryption, Block Heat Assessment	Blockchain Storage Efficiency	Optimizes encryption and block storage for privacy and cost-effectiveness.
Liu, Liang & Lyu, 2024	SSI Creation System with Blockchain	ZKP, Multi-party Audit, Blockchain Signatures	Self-Sovereign Identity (SSI)	Enhances SSI with privacy-preserving cross-domain data sharing.

2.2.4 Specialised Applications of Blockchain Cryptography

Ajakwe et al. (2024)explored the most frequent security risks to medical records transmission, the latest security measures to ensure the protection of patient privacy, and the key preconditions of proper, transparent authentication and authorisation to transmit data. A systematic analysis of 122 research papers was conducted in the study using the PRISMA-SPIDER technique. Of these, 9 surveys (7.37%) were analyzed qualitatively, 109 were analyzed technically (89.34%), and 4 were analyzed quantitatively (3.27%). Although in its infancy, blockchain can still guarantee the following: unfettered owner authorisation, unwavering host preservation, untainted transmission transparency, impartial traceability and ubiquity security, which is indispensable in safeguarding the sensitivity and confidentiality of highly classified records, like Medical Records. To facilitate the secure and transparent storage, user access, and authentication procedures of the Medical Records before their transmission to third-party access, one should consider resolving the technological hiccups inherent in blockchain and develop constructs that can aid it toward digital medical record preservation[121].

In this research, Ratul, Mollajafari and Wynn (2024) proposed a blockchain-based application to secure and organise digital evidence in cases involving crimes in a context of technology. A proposed approach prepares the foundation of a novel paradigm with a consortium blockchain to enable safe collaboration among judges' grown-ups and ensure evidence admissibility in court and integrity. According to a comprehensive literature review, blockchain technology can be utilised to develop an evidence management system that is both more effective and secure. They installed a web interface, tested Smart Contracts, deployed a localised blockchain, and stored evidences off-chain in order to test and develop the suggested paradigm. It was then deployed on two test networks that simulate an actual blockchain, namely Polygon and Ethereum. The findings indicated that Polygons operating cost was reduced by 99.96% over Ethereum, enabling Polygon to scale to any point without compromising security. This research suggests that blockchain technology may significantly transform the criminal justice system by re-evaluating chain of custody standards and enhancing the trustworthiness and security of evidence management[122].

In this study, Dam et al. (2023)presented statistics about the number and the characteristics of published works, reviewed literature, outlined the most frequently used methodologies to date, described the current status of implementation, different implementation comparisons, and discussed possible future activities. These papers focused on important methods for digital signatures and public cryptography. The NIST in the US held a contest to choose the most qualified individual to represent the normative standard. Recent work has ported Digital Signature algorithms and PKE/KEM mechanisms to a wide range of hardware platforms and optimized them with respect to various metrics. The trend towards PQC research is becoming increasingly visible, as is the general cryptography industry trend, and is part of an increasing number of academic publications. Researchers in digital signatures and public-key cryptography, particularly for algorithms chosen by NIST, have a new and exciting opportunity thanks to the movement[123].

Weichbroth et al. (2023) sought to provide theoretical and empirical understandings of the security environment, with an emphasis on both technological fixes and aspects pertaining to people. They used an integrated review, which might help provide the groundwork for academic research and science by providing conceptual and empirical models. A combination of technological safeguards and individual efforts to better one's own knowledge, competence, talents, and social abilities is necessary for effective cyber attack defence. An exhaustive assessment of the most significant new innovations and accomplishments in the field of cryptocurrency security is provided by the results. The major concern should be the creation and execution of effective protections against social engineering assaults. Future study should investigate this matter further, especially considering the growing interest in digital currencies issued by central banks[124].

Alohali et al. (2023) introduced BDIE-AOFOLS, an algorithm for blockchain-driven image encryption that makes use of fractional-order Lorenz optimisation. The BDIE-AOFOLS approach incorporates the fractional Lorenz system, Tent Map, and Arnold Map via the FOLS method. To maximise PSNR, it also optimised the key generation process using an arithmetic optimisation method (AOA). The originality of the present study is defined by the development of an

AOA-based optimum key generation for the FOLS method. The BC could also securely store the cryptographic pixel values of the picture, making the photographs unbreakable. They evaluated the proposed BDIE-AOFOLS approach using benchmark colour photographs. A peak signal-to-noise ratio of 61.80 dB and a MSE of 0.0430 were the metrics used to determine that the BDIE-AOFOLS approach outperformed the alternatives in terms of protecting sensitive information[125].

Vanin et al. (2023)advocated a design for infrastructure development that utilises a DHT method called the interplanetary protocol file system to separate metadata and data storage and distribution, and which also includes blockchain networks, data steward, and a shared data vault. The new components encourage end-to-end encryption and separate duties amongst healthcare institutions. As a result, data encryption, requests for data sharing, and temporary data access restrictions may all be managed by one individual. The following is an overview of their contributions beyond just making encrypted data calculations easier: (i) diminishing the danger to individual privacy via decreasing an employ of decrypted data, and (ii) enhancing healthcare institutions' semantic interoperability via the use of dispersed networks for standardising PHR, with the added provision of encrypted data computations. Through data analysis of storage utilisation and performance using a database including 1.3 million COVID-19 registrations, they demonstrated that new e-health paradigms may be developed by combining FHE with distributed networks[126].

In this study, Zubaydi, Varga and Molnár (2023) provided an in-depth evaluation of state-of-the-art BCT and IoT integration tactics, with a focus on resolving specific privacy and security issues. Topics covered in the study include the design, protocols, consensus processes, attributes, and integration issues of BCT and the IoT, among others. Next, the methodology section delves into every aspect of the survey, covering everything from the Search Strategy and eligibility requirements to the conclusions of the selection process and the study's included components. The results of the research are then shown, highlighting several projects that have tackled privacy and security issues by combining Blockchain

Technology with the IoT. Primary data, purpose, current development status, intended use case, blockchain and platform type, consensus algorithm, assessment metrics, assessment settings, work status (pending or completed), and any other pertinent remarks are used to further organise the apps that are being investigated. In addition, any and all studies, from an architectural and operational standpoint, are thoroughly discussed. Last but not least, they discuss important open questions and potential future directions for blockchain and IoTintegration[127].

Musa et al. (2023) began by outlining the state of the art in the topic and pointing out important gaps in the existing literature. Their dedication to Android is justified by its commanding share of the mobile market. They also devote space to discussing blockchain's development over time and how it relates to the security of current mobile apps. They learn a lot by looking at how different encryption methods work and how well blockchain protects data stored in mobile apps. They talk about the real-world effects of blockchain technology and how it improves upon other conventional forms of encryption. The BSADS architecture, which currently includes six complete levels, is the main contribution of this study. They provide technological optimisation solutions to problems with data Storage Costs, scalability, performance, and mobile-specific limitations. In an effort to be truthful and provide a whole picture, they are honest about the study's weakness. Along with outlining future prospects, they stress the significance of using lightweight nodes, fixing scalability problems, incorporating new technology, improving user experiences, and meeting regulatory standards[128].

Chen et al. (2023) the Hadoop distributed file system as the foundation for an approach to encrypted storage that is both easy to use and secure, EStore. Online distributed file systems would allow users to work together. After being uploaded and shared, most data is processed and kept in plaintext, making it impossible for the owner to manage it. While basic encryption ensures that submitted data remains private, it also makes the data less accessible. In addition, the issue of a single key encrypting several files raises the danger of leakage and makes complicated key management difficult to handle. They proposed a threat model and an encrypted storage model to address the aforementioned problems, along with a system architecture that could handle both. In addition, they created and deployed six sets of protocols to address the safety and usability concerns of users. Secure data outsourcing and searchable encryption/decryption modules were developed by EStore to manage users and their keys. These modules would only slightly increase the client's calculation overhead and storage redundancy, and they would allow for ciphertext retrieval. When contrasted with the initial file system, users are completely safe. As a last step, they demonstrated EStore's feasibility and security by doing a security analysis of the protocols[129].

Zhou et al. (2023) designed a two-sided approach to concerns with spatiotemporal big data. This paper is initiated on a proposal to split and scatter space-time big data, and this would permit encrypted and non-encrypted activities contingent upon the type of data. The confidential information exchange takes place with the help of smart contract technology. Additionally, CSSoB has better read than write performance, as shown in data that tested its single-node storage both locally and within a LAN. Reading and writing speed to files were also notably faster with larger files. Lastly, CSSoB and HDFS were compared by the number of transactions per second (TPS) at various thread counts. In example, CSSoB beat HDFS by 7.8 percentage points in TPS when the threads were placed at 100. The implementation of CSSoB could significantly enhance storage performance and security because of its high level of performance. Also, the fragmentation processing technology that is employed in this research enhances spatiotemporal data processing, secure data storage, and fast data querying[130].

Lin (2023) an advanced three-tiered blockchain architecture was created to ensure the safety of data in the IoV. To guarantee trader identification and non-repudiation of transactions, the paper proposes a new transaction block and uses ECDSA. The proposed multi-level blockchain design optimises the block overall by distributing tasks across intra-cluster and inter-cluster blockchains. It is possible to recover the system key on the cloud computing platform by collecting a certain number of partial keys, according to the threshold key management protocol. As a result, a PKI single-point failure is avoided. The security of OBU-RSU-BS-VM is therefore guaranteed by the suggested design. A block, an intra-cluster, and an interclusterBlockchain make up the three levels of the multi-level Blockchain Architecture that has been suggested. Local vehicle communication is handled by the Roadside Unit (RSU), which functions similarly to a cluster head in the IoV. The research entails using RSU for block management and the Base Stations for intra-cluster blockchain management (intra-cluster BC). Everything related to the system's blockchain is handled by the backend cloud server, which is referred to as inter_clusterBC. One final step towards enhancing blockchain operation security and efficiency is the coordinated development of multi-level blockchain architecture by RSUs, Base Stations, and cloud servers. The authors suggest a new structure for transaction blocks and use ECDSA to ensure the legitimacy and non-repudiation of transaction records while also forbidding manipulation of the Merkle Tree Root value in order to safeguard the blockchain's transaction data [87].

In this research, Pereira et al. (2023) discussed in depth the possible installation of a blockchain-based Voting System. A proposed system utilised cryptography in order to provide verifiable, and unchanged election results and voter privacy and anonymity. Digital Signatures, HE, ZKPs, and the ByzantineFault-Tolerant Consensus mechanism are system building blocks. To assess the technical and logistical challenges of implementing the proposed system, it is useful to review the literature on Blockchain Technology in connection to voting systems. The research offers answers to questions including how to handle scalability, network latency, voter verification, and accessibility. This proposed blockchain-based voting system could ensure privacy, anonymity and verifiability of the election outcomes, and could serve as a transparent and secure platform of voting and counting. The great degree of integrity and traceability offered by Blockchain Technology suggests it may solve the security and transparency issues with conventional voting methods[131].

He and Feng (2023) presented a way to handle the security challenges discussed earlier by leveraging the Ethernet blockchain within a cloud computing setting to accomplish verified fuzzy keyword queries in a manner that safeguards user confidentiality. The user could use the immutability properties of the Ethereum blockchain system to make sure that the query document is faithful and unmodified in this design. This would avert improper query results by the cloud server. Moreover, a just exchange between the server in the cloud and the user of the data is accomplished, and even in the event that either the user or the cloud is evil, it is possible to identify them via the use of hash functions and Ethereum Smart Contracts. As a conclusion, the security study demonstrates that their solution meets the semantic security requirements of the adaptive selection keyword when evaluated using the random oracle model. When compared to similar methods, the suggested one is more computationally efficient, according to the performance evaluation[132].

Lalem et al. (2023) provide an alternative method of Digital Signatures that is specific to a set of encryption techniques. The plan deals with both public and secret keys but specifically focusing on the former. The verification procedure involved multiplying the two parts so as to rebuild the PublicKey of the sender, and then comparing that output to the ciphertext. Data integrity is ensured by checking the encrypted message, and authenticity is established by using the signer's PublicKey.Compared with other modern approaches, the proposed system runs the full signature task (signing and verification) in a smaller period of time.The study demonstrated its resistance to forgery and attacks on the recovery of its private keys. The presentation of complexity and robustness measurements of the execution of the proposed scheme showed promising statistics. These results demonstrated that the suggested method for signature verification and generation is efficient and successful[133].

In this study, Qin and Zhang (2023) suggested a novel, comprehensive approach for biometric picture encryption and decryption, which incorporates signature and authentication, by use of a layered 3D Arnold Transform algorithm. Moreover, the ElGamal Digital Signature is adopted to check the signature and ElGamal Encryption Algorithm is adopted in encryption. The concept is made up of the Arnold Transform and the PublicKey Cryptosystem two completely functional and user-friendly tools of key transmission. At this point, the approach protects user privacy by encrypting and securing biometric image authentication. Several experiments have been carried out to prove that the suggested model is both feasible and secure; it has also been compared to current encryption techniques to see which one produces better results. Storage, Transmission, and Authentication of Biometric Data for everyday usage might also be included in the suggested architecture[134].

Jiang, Sun and Feng (2022) presented a data transaction protection method that uses BlockchainTechnology to ensure the safe exchange of data. This study accomplishes the following goals:(1) identify data security and transaction protection issues in current data transaction models;(2) create a blockchain-based data transaction platform independent of third parties;(3) safeguard user data using a combination of Advanced Encryption Standard (AES) and improved HE technology; and (4) Store Encrypted data in the IPFS for distributed storage. Finally, they use IPFS's robust features in conjunction with various security verification procedures for data transactions, such as zero-knowledge proof, two-way authentication, and the unintentional transmission protocol. They want to keep optimising it for future efficiency gains as the security research shows that this technique provides stronger security with the same amount of time overhead[135].

Pilares et al. (2022) After reviewing 65 different EHR systems, it became clear that health organisations have fourteen big obstacles that must be overcome in order to lessen the risk and friction they face. These included things like simplicity of use, storage, ownership, validity, accessibility, scalability, interoperability, secrecy, security, and privacy. They provide HER Chain, a novel structure that is both meant to accomplish the first goal and tackles all the stated obstacles in the process. Consortium blockchains provide the decentralisation of patient data, while IPFS enables distributed storage, due to Hyperledger Sawtooth-based dual-blockchain topologies[136].

AlFaw, Elmedany and Sharif (2022) referenced a number of earlier research papers that examined blockchain security risks and proposed solutions to those risks. Even if the blockchain system is vulnerable to security breaches, there have been studies on the topic, but no comprehensive analysis of the problem. The research approach used in this study was observational. This approach has been used to carry out a great deal of study on blockchain vulnerabilities and threats. The research's conclusions seek to pinpoint the biggest security risks that blockchain technology faces while also taking security flaws into account. Methods and processes for handling security issues are investigated. The academic difficulties and restrictions of corporate security are discussed in this paper. In order to provide the groundwork for further research on blockchain-based security, this evaluation will act as a reference and platform[137].

In this study, Adee and Mouratidis (2022) developed to provide a framework for the encrypted storage of data in the cloud, therefore addressing current privacy and security issues such as data corruption, loss, and theft. They tracked out the source of the problem by perusing a wide range of articles on present cloud computing security frameworks. The research methodology used in this examination was derived from the domain of design science. Design science research methodologies include requirements elicitation, problem identification, artefact design and development, demonstration, and assessment. A combination of design thinking and Python was used to construct the artefact. Tables, algorithms, and histograms illustrate its utility. This research presents a four-step method for protecting sensitive information, which includes the following: identity-based encryption, Least Significant Bit Steganography, AES, and Rivest-Shamir-Adleman. The four steps consist of recovering and backing up data, exchanging data, using steganography, and encryption technologies. The suggested method safeguards cloud data from unauthorised access while simultaneously increasing its efficiency, redundancy, and security[138].

In this research, Ali et al. (2022) proposed as a distributed database, safe search, and keyword-based access rely on a homomorphic encryption mechanism. Revocation of keys is also proposed, and the recommended approach provides a safe means of revoking keys. This led to the development of a trust chain and blockchain-based secure patient healthcare data access system that fixes the inefficiencies and security flaws in the existing systems. Consequently, their proposed approach is affordable and safer, faster, and fairer. They used the blockchain-based technology Hyperledger Fabric and assessment and analysis platform Origin Lab to conduct their simulations. Their proposed results were compared to those of the benchmark models. The findings of their comparison reveal that their proposed framework, with its searchable feature and closed-bearable security, can be useful to the healthcare system[139].

Alshahrani (2022) developed a new encryption scheme of e-learning (EL) blockchain implementation, the aim of which was to improve the transparency of assessment processes. Their method can facilitate the simplification of tests and issue certification. Content neutrality and analytical capabilities were added to highlight the benefits of a blockchain back-end, especially in the COVID-19 era. The use of SC and blockchain in online education is detailed in this study. An IECCA is proposed for data encryption and decryption with the aim of enhancing assessment confidence. It compares the suggested method's performance to that of other known encryption algorithms in order to assess its efficacy. The research found that the suggested method would boost trust in online classrooms, assessments, student data, and credentials[140].

Ahmed et al. (2022) conducted a comprehensive literature analysis of recent scholarly articles and commercial products on the topic of BC-based SSI solutions. It presents an exhaustive, chronological review of IDMS solutions and Blockchain Technology. The five essential features of a BC-based IDMS are laid forth in this study: trust, simplicity, authenticity, and integrity. They want to build a successful system that focuses on safeguarding a user's SSI. Furthermore, via security research, they discover several hostile threat kinds that might impair the BC-based IDMS. Through a review of the literature on several prominent BC-based IDMS systems, they are able to identify and talk about related problems and difficulties. They also highlight any gaps in our present understanding and outline the breadth of future research[72].

R. Alagheband and Mashatan (2022) intended to hasten the uptake of sophisticated DigitalSignatures. They serve as a link between the applied IoT systems and the sophisticated theoretical digital signatures that have lately been created in research focused on cryptography. It helps researchers achieve more privacy, security, and certain special features. To start, they show how Blockchain

Technology may be utilized in conjunction with an end-to-end, fog-to-cloud, and hierarchical IoT architecture to its advantage. Secondly, in order to cater to entities in IoT systems, their study takes a look at five cutting-edge digital signature schemes: randomizable, keyless, subitizable, and redactable. Among the many resources provided are taxonomy, an overview, a comparison table, and several use cases using the IoT. Researchers may use the integration of primitives and connection diagrams to their advantage when selecting sophisticated Digital Signatures, which they can then apply to a variety of IoT entities for the purpose of managing trust and protecting privacy[141].

Qureshi et al. (2022) offered computer and storage resources to customers on an as-needed basis with a pay-per-use model. It makes it possible for small firms to access affordable, high-quality infrastructure. Smart systems continually transmit data created to third-party managed cloud computing resources however; data privacy and security are major worries and obstacles owing to the cloud resource sharing feature. The problem of data security has prompted the proposal of many encryption methods. Presenting their operations visually, this study critically analyses and compares several current data security and encryption approaches that are based on common factors. This study aims to compile all existing literature on data encryption approaches, with a special emphasis on those that address the topic of transferring smart system data security to the cloud[142].

Adeniyi et al. (2022) improved safety and confirmed the transfer of private data via the use of RSA and ElGamal cryptographic techniques in conjunction with the use of SHA-256 for Digital Signature generation. As time goes on, it becomes more and more difficult to meet security criteria. This work aims to integrate cryptographic methods with the SHA-256 algorithm after authenticate shared data. The ElGamal and RSA cryptographic algorithms were built in C#, and the SHA-256 hash function was used to establish a Digital Signature. According to the results of the experiments, RSA is better at encrypting and signature verification, whereas ElGamal is better at creating and decrypting signatures[143].

Ahmed and Barukab (2022) proposed a method to fix the Diffie-Hellman exchange's bad bit issue by including an irreversible digital signature into a lightweight encryption system that relies on the ECDH secure key distribution. An unsafe communication channel between Internet of Things devices may be securely extended using the ELCD mechanism's proposed method of blending Digital Signatures and encryption, which involves using rapid hash functions. Lastly, the ELCD procedure uses a digital signature that includes three steps of curve point analysis and a hash function to confirm the sender's identity. The mathematical proof of ELCD's security was further supported by the use of the random oracle and models of IoT adversaries. Based on the simulation findings, ELCD is more efficient than the baseline cryptographic methods according to CPU Execution Time (53.8% reduction), StorageCost (33-17% reduction), and Power Consumption (68.7% reduction)[144].

Sintyaningrum, Muladi and Ashar (2021) sought to improve the security system by using QR codes and digital signatures to verify users and validate certificates, reducing instances of certificate counterfeiting. Users may use the program whenever and wherever they choose since it is incorporated into a web system. This study's end product is an innovative program that facilitates the online publication and validation of electronic authenticity certificates. The system's two primary schemes are the one for creating electronic certificates and the one for verifying QR Codes. A digital signature and a QR Code are necessary for an electronic professional certificate application. It has the potential to publish an electronic certificate that, when tested and proved in practice, might deter illicit activities like certificate counterfeiting[145].

Gupta, Gupta and Shukla (2021) introduced a novel session key-based, low-power encryption technique for digital photos. This study investigates a whole new session key. Crossover and Chebyshev map hybrids are used to generate session keys. When encrypting data, the crossover process is often used to maximise confusion and dispersion. This technique utilises an 80-bit key and 64-bit plaintext; the latter is generated at random using a provided symmetric hexadecimal key, while the former is derived from a fixed source. By combining the Chebyshev map with the crossover to generate a session key that is more difficult to predict, the proposed technique enhances security[146].

Takieldeen et al. (2021)a combination of ECC and two additional schemes—the OSS signature system and chaotic maps—to form a hybrid identity authentication pipeline. The latter option provides the necessary assurance and safety. A reversible matrix is inferred to form part of the OSS signature equation using cyclic group and chaotic mapping, and a substitution box (S-Box), which is the new feature of the methodology. The ECC-based security component is a computationally efficient PublicKeyCryptography technique that is the most feasible way to authenticate and ensure privacy on IoT devices. The proposed scheme is robust in that it incorporates IFP and DLP. The suggested method has been tested in a Lab-View environment and contrasted with other cutting-edge technologies. Its resilience to several attack types, including linear and differentiable assaults, was shown by a thorough analysis of simulation results, time rendering results, and security. The following table 2.4 provide the summary of related work on Specialized Blockchain Cryptography Applications[147].

Table 2.4: Summary of Related Works on Specialized Blockchain Cryptography Applications.

Author(s), Year	Proposed System/Model	Techniques Used	Focus Area	Key Contributions/ Outcomes
Ajakwe et al., 2024	Systematic Blockchain Review for Medical Records	PRISMA-SPIDER, Literature Analysis	Medical Data Security	Highlights blockchain's role in privacy, transparency, and traceability of medical records.
Ratul, Mollajafari and Wynn, 2024	Blockchain for Digital Evidence Management	Smart Contracts, Polygon & Ethereum	Legal Tech/Criminal Justice	Ensures evidence admissibility and secure chain-of-custody with reduced costs via Polygon.
Dam et al., 2023	Post-Quantum Cryptography Review	Digital Signature Algorithms, NIST PQC	Cryptographic Trends	Reviewed PQC trends, NIST-selected algorithms, and hardware implementations.
Weichbroth et al., 2023	Security Perspectives in Cryptocurrency	Integrated Review, Conceptual Models	Crypto Security	Emphasizes technical + human safeguards and future research on

				social engineering attacks.
Alohali et al., 2023	BDIE-AOFOLS Image Encryption	FOLS, Tent Map, Arnold Map, AOA, PSNR	Image Encryption	High-performance image encryption with optimized key generation and low MSE.
Vanin et al., 2023	Distributed Metadata for Healthcare	IPFS, FHE, Shared Data Vault	Healthcare Data Management	Enhances semantic interoperability and encrypted data sharing using decentralized storage.
Zubaydi, Varga and Molnár, 2023	Blockchain-IoT Integration Survey	Survey, App Classification, Metrics	Blockchain-IoT	Comprehensive review on privacy/security apps integrating blockchain with IoT.
Musa et al., 2023	BSADS for Mobile Blockchain Security	Six-layer Architecture, Android, Lightweight Nodes	Mobile Security	Proposes secure and optimized blockchain security architecture for mobile applications.
Chen et al., 2023	EStore Encrypted Storage Model	HDFS, Searchable Encryption, Protocol Stack	Cloud Storage	Enables secure encrypted file storage with minimal overhead and ciphertext retrieval.
Zhou et al., 2023	CSSoB for Spatiotemporal Data	Smart Contracts, Fragmentation Processing	Big Data Storage	Improves storage performance and secure access for spatiotemporal big data.
Lin, 2023	3-Level Blockchain for IoV	ECDSA, Intra/Inter-cluster Blockchain, Threshold Key Mgmt	Internet of Vehicles	Enhances vehicle data exchange with a scalable, secure multi-level blockchain architecture.
Pereira et al., 2023	Blockchain-Based Voting System	ZKP, Homomorphic Encryption, Digital Signatures	E-voting	Provides secure, verifiable, and anonymous blockchain voting framework.
He and Feng, 2023	Ethereum-based Fuzzy	Smart Contracts,	Cloud Security	Ensures verifiable, private queries

	Keyword Search	Fuzzy Search, Hash Verification		using blockchain's immutability and mutual trust mechanisms.
Lalem et al., 2023	Lightweight Digital Signature Scheme	Public Key Encryption, Ciphertext Matching	Digital Signature & Data Integrity	Fast signature operations, strong authenticity, resistance to forgery, reduced execution time.
Qin & Zhang, 2023	Layered Biometric Data Encryption	3D Arnold Transform, ElGamal Encryption & Signature	Biometric Image Protection	Secure biometric data handling with layered encryption; improved encryption security and authentication.
Jiang, Sun & Feng, 2022	Blockchain-based Data Transaction Platform	AES, Homomorphic Encryption, IPFS, ZKP, 2FA	Secure Data Sharing	Eliminates third parties, secures data with advanced encryption, adds IPFS for distributed storage.
Pilares et al., 2022	HER Chain for EHR Systems	Dual Blockchain, Hyperledger Sawtooth, IPFS	EHR Storage & Interoperability	Addresses 14 major EHR system issues; decentralised, secure, and scalable.
AlFaw, Elmedany & Sharif, 2022	Blockchain Security Risk Evaluation	Observational Risk Analysis	Blockchain Vulnerability Assessment	Summarises risks and threats; identifies research gaps; proposes foundational insights for further research.
Adee & Mouratidis, 2022	Secure Cloud Storage Framework	AES, RSA, Steganography, Design Science	Cloud Security & Data Privacy	Four-step model for secure cloud data storage using hybrid encryption and steganography.
Ali et al., 2022	Blockchain Patient Data Access	Homomorphic Encryption, Hyperledger Fabric	Healthcare Data Access	Secure, searchable, revocable access to patient records; cost-effective and efficient.
Alshahrani, 2022	E-Learning Blockchain System	IECCA Encryption, Smart Contracts	Education & Assessment	Enhances test transparency, credential validation, and academic trust.

Ahmed et al., 2022	BC-based Self-Sovereign Identity System	Literature Synthesis, Threat Analysis	Identity Management	Defines 5 key features for BC-IDMS; identifies attacks and future scopes in SSI.
Alagheband & Mashatan, 2022	IoT Digital Signature Adoption Framework	Advanced Signature Types, Fog-to-Cloud IoT	IoT Trust Management	Taxonomy of advanced digital signatures for IoT; enhances privacy, security, and flexibility.
Qureshi et al., 2022	Smart System Cloud Encryption Review	Encryption Scheme Comparison	Cloud Offloading & Data Privacy	Analyses several methods for securing data during offloading to cloud services.
Adeniyi et al., 2022	Secure File Sharing Framework	RSA, ElGamal, SHA-256	Secure Communication	RSA excels at verification; ElGamal efficient at encryption; ensures digital signature authentication.
Ahmed & Barukab, 2022	ELCD Lightweight IoT Encryption	ECDH, SHA-256, Hash Functions	IoT Encryption & Key Management	High security with reduced CPU use (53.8%), storage (33–17%), and power (68.7%).
Sintyaningrum et al., 2021	Certificate Validation System	QR Code, Digital Signature, Waterfall SDLC	Certificate Anti-Forgery	Online certificate validation system to prevent counterfeiting using QR and digital signature.
Gupta, Gupta & Shukla, 2021	Lightweight Session Key Encryption	Chebyshev Map, Crossover, Session Key Generation	Image Security	Secure image encryption with small key/code footprint; MATLAB-tested.
Takieldeen et al., 2021	Hybrid Identity Authentication Scheme	Chaotic Maps, OSS Signature, ECC, S-Box	IoT Authentication	Combines strong cryptographic layers; high attack resistance; verified in LabView.

2.3 Research Gap

Although there are sufficient innovations in the sphere of blockchain-based cryptographic systems, there are specific research gaps that remain to be filled, especially when it comes to applying self-signed keys to encrypt digital records. Most existing systems rely heavily on centrally controlled certificate authorities or outsourced services to achieve security by means of third-party key validation and identity verification, which compromises the very core decentralization principle that blockchain was invented to support. The applicability of self-signed keys and the resulting ability to achieve decentralized trust is not well considered in the context of blockchain ecosystems, particularly in what ways trustworthiness and authenticity can be achieved even in the absence of hierarchical trust. Additionally, more rigorous structures that could facilitate secure, lightweight, scalable encryption processes favourable in resource-restrained situations such as the IoT and mobile health care networks are not present. The majority of current research is done on the encryption methods or key management individually, without the idea of a combined system that includes encryption and authentication, access control and secure sharing of data using blockchain. Moreover, the increasing problem of quantum computer adoption also adds to this issue, but the combination of post-quantum cryptographic techniques and self-signed key-based techniques is only just in its early stages. There is also little real-world study on performance, latency, and energy consumption of blockchain systems using self-signed keys under high-demand conditions. Such gaps reveal the necessity of a full-fledged decentralized cryptographic system that uses self-signed keys harmoniously with blockchain to increase data security, privacy as well as trust, particularly in delicate areas like healthcare, finance, and identity management. The following key research gaps are:

- Most existing blockchain systems rely on centralized or third-party key validation services, which contradict the core principle of decentralization.
- There is insufficient exploration of how decentralized trust can be achieved using self-signed keys in blockchain environments without hierarchical or centralized trust structures.

- Current research often addresses encryption, authentication, or access control in isolation, rather than integrating them into a cohesive, secure blockchain-based framework.
- There is a scarcity of lightweight, scalable cryptographic approaches suitable for environments such as IoT and mobile healthcare networks.
- There has been no research examining the practical implementation of combining self-signed key methods with post-quantum cryptography algorithms.
- Few studies evaluate blockchain systems using self-signed keys under real-world constraints, like high transaction loads, latency, and energy consumption.
- To address the unique privacy and legal concerns of industries like as healthcare and finance, there has been very little effort to modify blockchain-based cryptography systems using self-signed keys.

The proposed study fills these knowledge gaps by presenting a blockchain-based decentralised system that uses self-signed ECC keys to do away with dependence on centralised authority. It integrates lightweight hybrid encryption, access control, and authentication into a unified architecture, optimized for resource-constrained environments like IoT and healthcare, while ensuring scalability, security, and readiness for post-quantum enhancements with real-world performance considerations.

CHAPTER - 3

RESEARCH METHODOLOGY

CONTENTS

Research publications

Advancements in Blockchain Cryptography: Self-Signed Key Applications for Digital Record Protection

Maheshwari, P., Gupta, S., (2025). "Advancements in Blockchain Cryptography: Self-Signed Key Applications for Digital Record Protection", Journal of Applied Engineering and Technological Science, Volume: 6, Issue: 2, pp: 1215 – 1236. DOI: 10.37385/jaets.v6i2.6335

A Novel Decentralized Cryptographic Approach for Robust Authentication of Financial Digital Records Using Blockchain

Maheshwari, P., Gupta, S., (2025). "A Novel Decentralized Cryptographic Approach for Robust Authentication of Financial Digital Records Using Blockchain". Journal of Information Systems Engineering and Management, Volume: 10, Issue: 33. DOI: 10.52783/jisem.v10i33s.5572

3.1 Overview

Cyber security threats, like data breaches, fraud, and unauthorized access, have emerged in tandem with the fast digitalization of the healthcare and finance industries, which has transformed data management and service delivery. Inadequate key management and single points of failure are only two of the many ways in which traditional centralized systems are falling short. This research suggests a hybrid encryption method that integrates blockchain technology with self-signed key cryptography and other existing methods to circumvent these restrictions. Data confidentiality, integrity, and authenticity are guaranteed across financial transactions and healthcare records by using blockchain's decentralized, irreversible nature with sophisticated cryptographic technologies. In addition to improving the security of digital data, this strategy provides a transparent, scalable, and trust-based solution for safe digital infrastructure, establishing the groundwork for robust systems in the banking, healthcare, and other industries.

3.2 Problem Formulation

In today's digital landscape, both the financial and healthcare sectors are experiencing a surge in data generation and digital service delivery, making them prime targets for cyberattacks, data breaches, and fraudulent activities. Financial institutions face increasing threats to the confidentiality and integrity of transaction data due to the shift towards online and mobile banking, often compounded by challenges related to scalability, regulatory compliance, and secure cloud-based communication. Similarly, healthcare systems are struggling to protect sensitive patient information, with existing centralized architectures proving inadequate for ensuring data authenticity, privacy, and traceability. The absence of safe, decentralized system that can authenticate users in real time and store data without tampering making vulnerabilities worse.

To address these issues, this study proposes the formulation of a comprehensive, cross-domain security framework that integrates blockchain technology with self-signed key cryptography and hybrid encryption techniques. For the financial sector, the system uses dual-layer encryption (AES and DES) along with pseudo-random key generation securely stored on a blockchain to protect transaction data. For the healthcare sector, self-signed cryptographic keys generated using Elliptic Curve Cryptography (ECC) are used to sign and authenticate medical records before recording them immutably on a blockchain ledger. Scalable, decentralised, and tamper-resistant solutions that improve trust, interoperability, and security in both healthcare and financial infrastructures are the goals of this dual-application approach, which seeks to overcome the constraints of present systems.

3.3 Need for the Study

In an increasingly digitized world, both the financial and healthcare sectors generate vast volumes of sensitive data that require stringent security and privacy measures. Common problems with traditional centralised systems include lack of transparency, vulnerability to illegal access or data manipulation, and single points of failure. Financial institutions face rising incidents of fraudulent transactions, while healthcare systems grapple with breaches of confidential patient information. These threats not only compromise data integrity but also erode public trust and can lead to severe legal and economic consequences. As such, there is a pressing need to adopt innovative technologies that provide stronger data protection, real-time access control, and transparent audit trails.

Blockchain technology, when combined with advanced cryptographic methods such as self-signed key authentication and hybrid encryption, offers a robust solution to these challenges. Secure data transfer and storage is guaranteed by its cryptographic procedures, and records cannot be changed once certified by its decentralised and immutable ledger. This study seeks to leverage these technologies to develop secure, decentralized frameworks tailored to both financial transaction protection and healthcare data security. By doing so, it aims to provide a scalable and reliable model that can significantly reduce fraud, enhance data integrity, and build greater confidence in digital systems across critical sectors.

3.4 Novelty in Method

This research is groundbreaking because it tackles the twin problems of healthcare and financial data authenticity and safe access by combining blockchain technology with self-signed key cryptography and hybrid encryption. Unlike conventional security frameworks that use static encryption or centralized key storage, this study proposes a decentralized and tamper-proof ledger where encryption keys and digital signatures are stored and validated in real time. The use of a dual encryption layer—combining AES and DES—adds an extra level of security for financial transaction data, while self-signed ECC-based keys provide lightweight yet highly secure authentication for healthcare records. This dual-application approach has not been widely explored, particularly with both sectors being secured through a common blockchain-backed infrastructure.

Furthermore, the application of self-signed cryptographic keys enhances the user's ability to maintain full control over data without relying on third-party certificate authorities. In addition to protecting the authenticity of each record, this method makes sure that no one other than authorised users may access private data. Blockchain technology provides an additional level of transparency and immutability by serving as a distributed ledger for encrypted data and key records. The combination of these elements—custom key generation, decentralized storage, dual-sector applicability, and cryptographic self-validation—marks a significant advancement over existing systems, presenting a forward-looking solution tailored for the secure digital transformation of critical sectors. The integrated approach of these technologies enhances the overall security and integrity of digital records. Digital authentication systems undergo a sea change as a result of this integration, opening the door to further evolutionary improvements in decentralised security solutions.

3.5 Proposed Methodology for Fraudulent Transaction Data Security

This section lays out the study's methodology, the dataset, and the methods utilised. This project aims to establish a trustworthy framework that uses blockchain technology and sophisticated encryption methods to identify and safeguard financial transaction data from fraudulent actions. The proposed methodology begins with the use of a publicly available Fraudulent Transaction dataset sourced from Kaggle, consisting of over 6.3 million records and spanning 30 days, where each transaction is characterized by features such as amount, balance details, transaction type, and fraud indicators. To secure this sensitive financial data, the methodology employs a hybrid encryption mechanism combining AES and DES algorithms, providing a dual-layered approach to encryption. A User Interface (UI) allows users to input data and initiate transactions, while the data access layer ensures secure storage and retrieval using encrypted connections. The key generation module creates unique keys using pseudo-random functions and timestamps, which are securely stored on a blockchain, ensuring immutability and protection against unauthorized access. The encryption module encrypts data sequentially with AES and DES, and the final encrypted data, along with hash values and metadata, is stored in a blockchain ledger for tamper-proof protection. The decryption module restores the original data using the corresponding keys, while a comprehensive security module ensures authentication, intrusion detection, and data integrity. Encrypted data is either stored on the blockchain or in a protected database or secure transmission protocols safeguard data movement within the system, forming a resilient framework against financial fraud. Figure 3.1 shows the methodology's flowchart below.

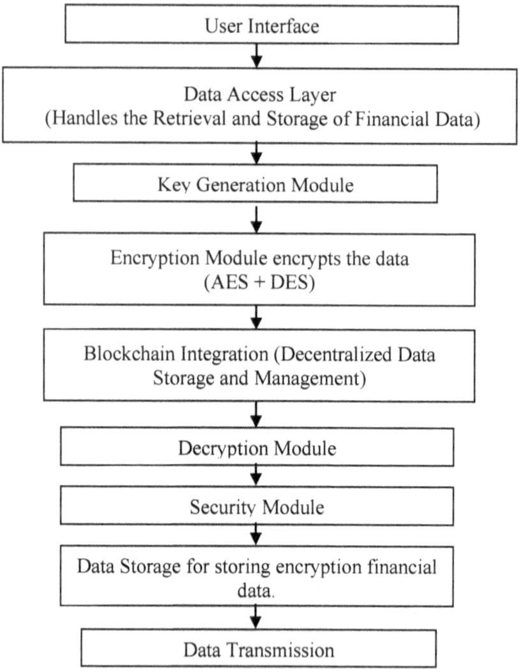

Figure 3.1: Proposed Methodology Flowchart for Secure and Reliable Framework for Detecting and Protecting Financial Transaction

The suggested technique for a safe and dependable framework intended for identifying and safeguarding financial transactions is shown in Figure 3.1. The UI, which allows people to engage with the system, is where the process starts. The Data Access Layer, which manages the retrieval and archiving of financial data, is the result of this interaction. Subsequently, a Key Generation Module is employed to generate cryptographic keys. The Encryption Module then uses these keys to encrypt the financial data, ensuring secrecy by using the AES and DES algorithms. Integrating Blockchain Technology allows for distributed and immutable data storage and administration after encryption, eliminating the need for a central authority. When the encrypted data needs to be accessed, it passes through a Decryption Module. A Security Module then provides additional layers of protection and integrity checks. Finally, the processed and secured financial data is directed to a dedicated Data Storage for encrypted financial data before it undergoes Data Transmission. This comprehensive flow aims to secure financial transactions from input to storage and transmission.

3.5.1 Dataset Description

The study utilized the publicly available Fraudulent Transaction dataset[1] from the Kaggle repository to develop a model for detecting fraud in financial transactions. The dataset is available in CSV format and comprises 6,362,620 records, each described by 10 features, and spans a simulated time frame of 30 days (744 steps, with each step representing one hour). The average transaction value is approximately $ 144,972 USD, while the maximum recorded transaction value is $ 1,991,430 USD. However, the dataset exhibits a heavily right-skewed distribution, where most transactions are of relatively small amounts, and only a small fraction approaches the upper limit. This dataset simulates real-world transaction patterns for a financial organisation, offering valuable insights into customer and account behaviours[148]. The features of the dataset include key transactional details e given in Table 3.1.

1 https://www.kaggle.com/datasets/chitwanmanchanda/fraudulent-transactions-data

Table 3.1: Dataset Description

Feature Name	Description
Step	Represents the unit of time in hours, where each step is equivalent to 1 hour over 30 days (744 steps).
Type	Specifies the transaction type, including CASH-IN, CASH-OUT, DEBIT, PAYMENT, and TRANSFER.
OldbalanceDest	The recipient's account balance prior to the transaction. For merchants (IDs starting with "M"), this data is unavailable.
NewbalanceOrig	The original account balance of the person whose funds were transferred after the transfer is completed.
oldbalanceOrg	The account balance of the transaction initiator before the transaction occurred.
NameOrig	A unique identity for the client who started the transaction.
NameDest	A unique identity for the client who received the transaction.
NewbalanceDest	The recipient's account balance after the transaction. For merchants (IDs starting with "M"), this data is unavailable.
Amount	Denotes the monetary value of the transaction in the local currency.
IsFlaggedFraud	Marks transactions exceeding a value of 200,000 as potentially fraudulent (1 for Flagged, 0 for Not Flagged).
IsFraud	Indicates the likelihood that the transaction was fraudulent; a value of 1 indicates fraud and 0 indicates non-fraud.

3.5.2 Techniques used

The methods used in this investigation are detailed below:

1) Blockchain Technology

Blockchain technology guarantees tamper-proof records by decentralizing and encrypting information across a network of nodes. The distributed nature of the system makes it more resistant to malicious assaults and single points of failure[149][150]. Smart contracts automate and implement agreements without intermediaries, thereby minimizing the chances for fraudulent activities or mistakes. The blockchain is a system used to store and manage distributed ledgers containing sensitive data in an open digital format that can be read by anyone, as shown in Figure 3.2. Data security across several industries is anticipated to be greatly enhanced by this technology [151].

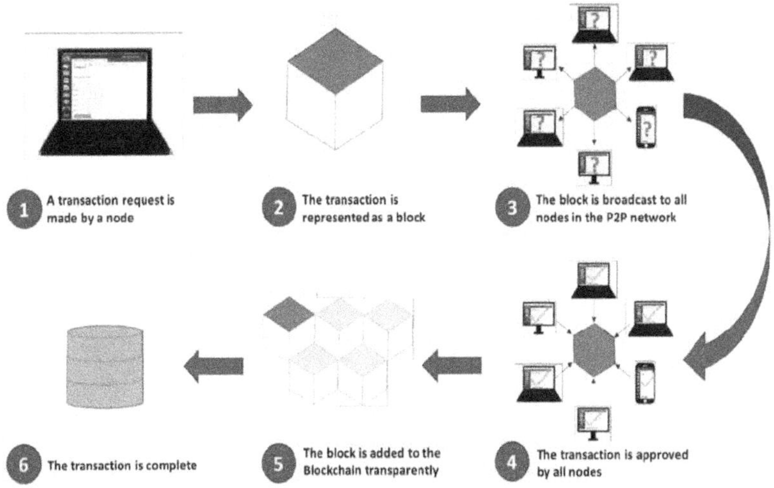

Figure 3.2: Working of Blockchain [152].

The blockchain is utilized in the context of this study to store encrypted financial data, ensuring the immutability, transparency, and security of the data. Besides, blockchain also plays a significant role in securely storing cryptographic keys or their hashes, which is crucial in encryption and decryption processes [153]. The distributed ledger technology of blockchain eliminates the possibility of unauthorised access to data or keys by making it very impossible to alter any record without coming to an agreement among network members.

3.5.3 Advanced Encryption Standard (AES)

The encryption module utilizes AES for securing data, which involves generating a random key of a specific length, such as 128 or 256 bits, that serves as the basis for encryption, as illustrated in Figure 3.3. With the assistance of such a key, the module utilizes the AES algorithm to encrypt the data. It does so based on fixed-size blocks[154]. This assumes that padding must be done since the size of the data may not correspond exactly to a multiple of the block size.

The AES decryption technique can only restore data from its encrypted state if the decryption keys are identical to the encryption keys[155]. Cryptographic key creation, distribution, storage, and rotation are all aspects of key management that are critical to protecting the privacy and integrity of encrypted data. Ensuring effective data protection requires strict attention to implementation best practices, even if AES encryption is recognised for its excellent security features and great efficiency[156].

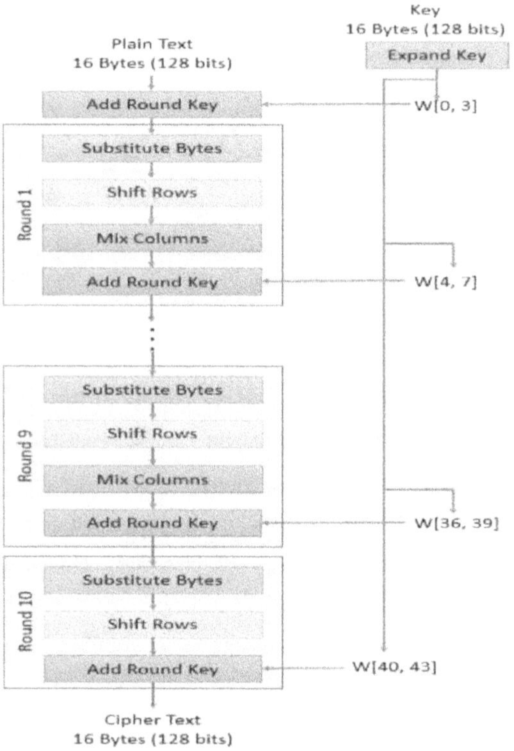

Figure 3.3: Advanced Encryption Standard (AES) [157].

Financial data is encrypted using AES as the first layer of security in this investigation. Ideal for protecting sensitive information, it works well and is resistant to common cryptographic assaults such differential cryptanalysis and brute force. Data security is greatly improved by AES's robust encryption, which makes data unintelligible without the decryption key, regardless of whether it is intercepted during transmission or storage[158].

3.5.4 Data Encryption Standard (DES)

DES is an example of symmetric-key algorithms commonly used in securing electronic information[159]. It starts with the creation of a 56-bit key within a typical DES encryption module, as shown in Figure 3.4. Additionally, there occurs an initial permutation on a 64-bit plaintext block followed by several rounds, usually sixteen using a Feistel network structure whereby each round utilizes a different subkey derived from the original key [160]. Combination substitution-permutation operations constitute these rounds. At the last stage, after the final round is over final permutation takes place, resulting in a 64-bit ciphertext block. To decrypt, the process is reversed using the same key in the opposite order [161].

However, DES is no longer recommended for usage in secure applications because to its vulnerability to brute-force attacks caused by its low key size[162][163]. Longer key lengths in modern encryption methods, like AES, are currently favoured for providing strong data security[164].

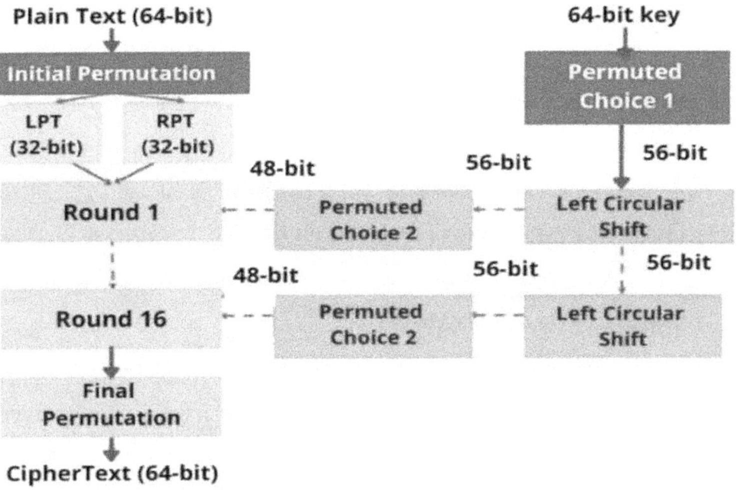

Figure 3.4: Data Encryption Standard.

In this study, DES is strategically combined with AES to create a dual-layered encryption mechanism. This approach improves data security through the Degrees of Freedom (DoF) introduced by DES, where multiple transformations and key dependencies diversify the encryption process. By using DES after AES, the system achieves additional cryptographic complexity, making it significantly harder for attackers to decrypt the data without both keys [165]. This data will be safe during transmission and storage because to the twofold encryption, which kicks in if one layer of encryption is cracked.

3.5.5 Proposed Algorithm for Financial Digital Records security using blockchain

Algorithm 1: Financial Digital Records security using blockchain

Start

Step 1: User Interface

UI Design:

Develop the user interface UI with input functionalities $F_{capture}(x)$, transaction initiations $F_{transact}(x)$, and access mechanism $F_{access}(x)$. It calculates as Equation 3.1:

$$UI = \{F_{capture}(x), F_{transact}(x), F_{access}(x)\} \quad ...(3.1)$$

Step 2: Data Access Layer

Database Connection:

Define data access functions $D_{retrieved}(q)$ for retrieval and $D_{store}(d)$ for storage. Ensure secure connections using protocols like TLS, calculates as Equation 3.2:

$$Secure\_Connection \implies TLS\_Handshake + K_{session} \quad ... (3.2)$$

Step 3: Key Generation Module

Key Combination Algorithm (AES + DES):

Generate unique keys K_{AES} and K_{DES}. Combine these using a pseudo-random function (PRF), calculates as Equation 3.3:

$$K_{combined} = PRF(K_{AES}, K_{DES}) \quad ... (3.3)$$

Ensure uniqueness using a timestamp T_i , calculates as Equation 3.4:

$$K_{final} = H(K_{combined}, T_i)4) \quad ... (3.4)$$

H is a cryptographic hash function.

Blockchain Key Storage:

Store keys securely using a blockchain where Hash(K) and metadata M are added to blocks, calculates as Equation 3.5:

$$B = \{Hash(K_{final}), M, Prev_{Hash}\} \quad .... (3.5)$$

Step 4: Encryption Module

AES + DES Encryption:

Encrypt data D using K_{final}, calculates as Equations 3.6 and 3.7:

$E_{AES} = AES(D, K_{AES})$

$E_{DES} = DES(E_{AES}, K_{DES})$

Final encrypted data, calculates as Equation 3.8:

$$D_{encrypted} = Combine(E_{AES}, E_{DES}) \quad ... (3.6)$$

Step 5: Blockchain Integration

Data Block Formation:

Encrypt data and form blockchain transactions T, calculates as Equation 3.9:

$$T = \{Hash(D_{encrypted}), Metadata, Prev\_Hash\} \quad ... (3.7)$$

Step 6: Decryption Module

Decryption Process:

Reverse encryption using K_{AES} and K_{DES}, calculates as Equation 3.10:

$$D_{decrypted} = AES^{-1}(DES^{-1}(D_{encrypted}, K_{DES})K_{AES}) \quad ...(3.8)$$

Step 7: Security Module

Authentication and Authorization:

Use a secure authentication mechanism with $H(U, P)$:, calculates as Equation 3.11

$$Auth_{user} = H(U, P) == Stored\_Hash(U) \quad (3.11)$$

Intrusion Detection:

Deploy an anomaly detection system A_{IDS} with thresholds T_a, calculates as Equation 3.12:

$$A_{\text{IDS}}(x) = \begin{cases} Alert\ if\ x > T_a \\ Allow\ if\ x \leq T_a \end{cases} \quad ... (3.12)$$

Step 8: Data Storage

Secure Storage:

Store $D_{\text{encrypted}}$ in either blockchain or a secure data repository. Blockchain ensures, calculates as Equation 3.13:

$$Immutability = Hash(B_i) == Stored\_Hash(B_i) \qquad ...(3.13)$$

Step 9: Data Transmission

Secure Transmission:

Transmit data using protocols like AES-encrypted channels, calculates as Equation 3.14:

$$D_{transmitted} = Encrypt(D_{encrypted}, K_{session}) \qquad ...(3.14)$$

End

3.5.6 Model Evaluation Parameters

This study's performance estimate is based on the following assessment metrics:

(i) Execution Time (T_{exec}):

Execution time measures the total time taken to complete a specific task or process in the system. It includes all processing stages, from data encryption to storage and retrieval. This is a crucial metric for assessing system efficiency. It calculates as Equation 3.15:

$$T_{exec} = T_{start} - T_{end} \qquad ...(3.15)$$

(ii) Average Latency (L_{avg}):

Latency refers to the delay experienced in the system when processing a single request. Average latency is the meantime taken across multiple requests, highlighting system responsiveness. It calculates as Equation 3.16:

$$L_{avg} = \frac{\sum_{i=1}^{N} L_i}{n} \qquad ...(3.16)$$

Where L_i is the latency for the i-th request, and n represents the sum of all requests.

(iii) Average Throughput (TP_{avg}):

"Throughput" describes how quickly a system can complete tasks or transactions. Average throughput evaluates the system's capacity to handle concurrent tasks efficiently. It calculates as Equation 3.17:

$$TP_{avg} = \frac{Total\ Transactions}{Total\ Time} \quad \text{... (3.17)}$$

(iv) Time Consumption (T_{cons}):

This metric calculates the overall amount of time the system needs to finish a number of operations, such as data transfer, key creation, and encryption. The value may be written as Equation 3.18:

$$T_{cons} = T_{enc} + T_{dec} + T_{upload} + T_{download} \quad \text{... (3.18)}$$

(v) Communication Cost (C_{comm}):

Communication cost represents the amount of resources (time, bandwidth, or data size) required for transmitting data between components. It is often measured in bytes or kilobytes transmitted per second. It calculates as Equation 3.19:

$$Ccomm = \frac{Data\ Transferred}{Bandwidt\ h} \quad \text{... (3.19)}$$

(vi) Key Generation Time (T_{key}):

This metric measures the time required to generate cryptographic keys using self-signed mechanisms, considering both the AES and DES algorithms. It calculates as Equation 3.20:

$$T_{key} = T_{AES\_key} + T_{DES\_key} \quad \text{... (3.20)}$$

(vii) Upload and Download Time (T_{upload}):

The time it takes to encrypt data, send it to the blockchain, and then retrieve it for decryption is quantified by these measures. It calculates as Equation 3.21:

$$T_{upload} = T_{initiate} + T_{process} + T_{store} \quad \text{... (3.21)}$$

(viii) Encryption Time (T_{enc}):

The time required to encrypt data using a hybrid encryption mechanism. It calculates as Equation 3.22:

$$T_{enc} = T_{AES_{enc}} + T_{DES_{enc}} \quad \text{... (3.22)}$$

(ix) Decryption Time (T_{dec}):

The time needed to decrypt the encrypted data back into its original form. It calculates as Equation 3.23:

$$T_{dec} = T_{DES\_dec} + T_{AES\_dec} \quad \text{... (3.23)}$$

The study's strategic justification for combining blockchain technology with AES and DES encryption enhance the security, transparency, and integrity of data pertaining to financial transactions. The data is safeguarded even if one layer of encryption is broken by using a dual-layer encryption scheme, which is especially important for financial records due to their highly sensitive nature and the rising incidence of cyber-attacks. AES offers high-speed encryption with strong resistance to attacks, while DES adds an additional complexity layer, collectively improving cryptographic robustness. Blockchain further strengthens the system by providing a decentralized, immutable ledger that prevents unauthorized tampering and ensures traceability of all transactions and key usage. This combination not only safeguards data during storage and transmission but also ensures accountability, user authentication, and intrusion prevention. As a result, the proposed framework delivers a comprehensive, scalable, and tamper-resistant solution well-suited for modern financial systems requiring high levels of data confidentiality and integrity.

3.6 Proposed Methodology for Healthcare Data Security

An effective and safe system for securing electronic medical records utilising blockchain technology and self-signed key applications is the target of the proposed research. To achieve this, the study utilizes the publicly available MIMIC-III dataset, which contains anonymized medical data from over 40,000 patients, with a selected subset of 1,000 records used due to scalability and data handling constraints. Time stamps, medical histories, access logs, and patient IDs are all crucial components of these data. The approach calls for establishing a five-node blockchain network and validating transactions and data using a PoW consensus mechanism. A digital record structure is defined, and self-signed key pairs are generated using ECC with the secp256k1 curve, offering robust security with optimized performance. A private key is used to digitally sign each healthcare record, which is then hashed and added to the blockchain for verification purposes. Upon successful validation, the records are stored immutably in the distributed ledger, enabling secure, tamper-proof storage and real-time access by authorized users—thus ensuring traceability, confidentiality, and data integrity in the healthcare domain.

3.6.1 Dataset Description

The lack of freely accessible public datasets is a major obstacle for healthcare researchers. The public does not have easy access to healthcare data due to its sensitive nature. However, there is a finite quantity of anonymized datasets that may be accessed on the internet. The data records needed for the proposed study must include patient identifiers such name, date of birth, and other contact information. Anonymized datasets are thus unsuitable for the criteria. To address the above problems, the proposed study utilized the MIMIC-III dataset (https://www.kaggle.com/datasets/asjad99/mimiciii). The dataset is publicly available and includes medical information from more than 40,000 individuals who were hospitalized in critical care units at Beth Israel Deaconess Medical Centre between 2001 and 2012. The data has been anonymized to protect patient privacy. However, for the present experiment, this study employed just 1,000 records because of limitations in scalability and data management. This data collection approach supports the integration of blockchain cryptography, particularly self-signed keys making this an essential aspect of current research.

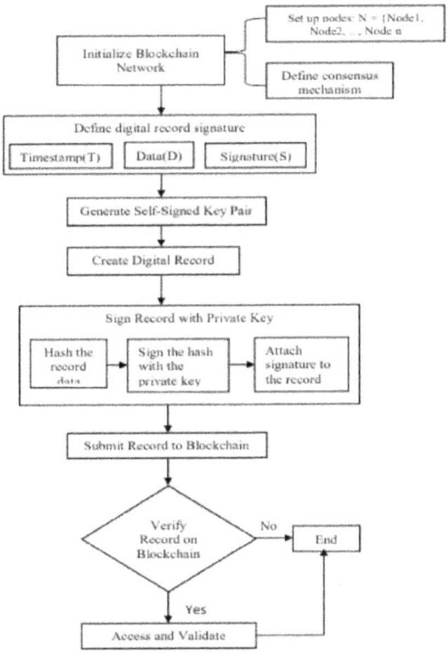

Figure 3.5: Proposed flowchart for secure healthcare dataset based on blockchain cryptography with self-signed key applications

Figure 3.5 illustrates the proposed flowchart for securing healthcare datasets using blockchain cryptography integrated with self-signed key applications. The process begins by initializing a blockchain network with multiple nodes and defining a consensus mechanism—specifically Proof of Work—to ensure trustworthy data validation. Next, the system establishes the digital record format comprising a timestamp, data, and signature. A self-signed key pair is generated using ECC, which is then used to create a digital record. The data is first hashed, then signed employing the private key, and finally the record is appended to the outcome of the signing procedure. This signed digital record is then submitted to the blockchain. The blockchain network verifies the record for authenticity and integrity. If verification fails, the process ends; otherwise, the record is securely stored on the immutable ledger, allowing authorized users to access and validate it in real time. This flow ensures confidentiality, data integrity, and tamper-proof recordkeeping in healthcare applications.

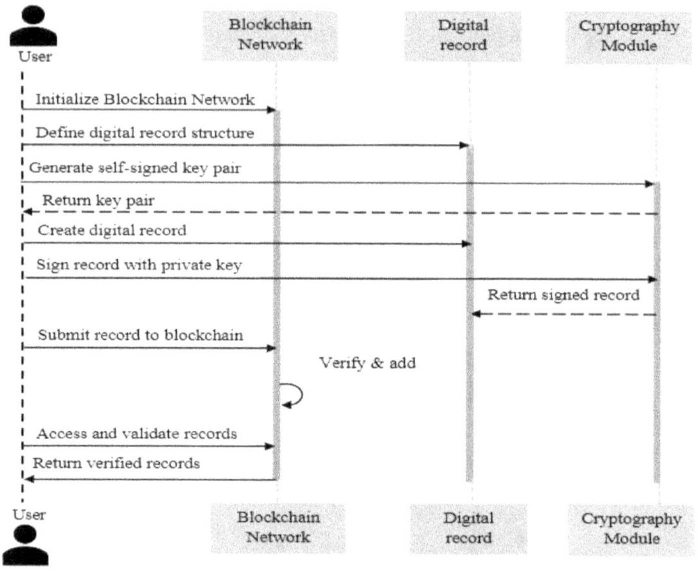

Figure 3.6: Proposed Sequence Diagram

The sequence diagram given in Figure 3.6 displays the interaction among the User, Blockchain Network, Digital Record, and Cryptography Module. The full workflow, from initializing the blockchain to the creation of self-signed key pairs, record generation, signing, and verification is depicted. The diagram also indicates the return of verified records, facilitating smooth and tamper-proof data handling. Moreover, the image perfectly depicts the sequential communication process between the modules concerning how the cryptography module produces and returns the signed record. It also illustrates the verification procedure carried out by the blockchain network before providing access to validated records. Such a comprehensive flow indicates the efficiency and security of the self-signed key mechanism in providing secure and tamper-proof digital record protection.

This method is employed for its scalability, security, and efficiency. ECC was particularly chosen for its high-speed processing and smaller key size compared to RSA, as it is most suitable for real-time blockchain applications. The use of self-signed keys eliminates the requirement for third-party certificate authorities, minimising external dependencies while providing increased privacy. The framework is benchmarked with emulated blockchain interactions, and 1000 transactions are processed to measure throughput, encryption/decryption time, and latency. Performance metrics, like Execution Time and transaction validation rate, are measured to determine the system's efficiency. The implementation utilizes Python for cryptography and Hyperledger Fabric for blockchain networking.

3.6.2 Initialising Blockchain Network

The installation of nodes, which are the fundamental components of a blockchain, is the first stage in constructing a blockchain network. Every node must be set to enable it to connect to the network through the distribution of distinct codes and defining the mode of communication, allowing nodes to communicate with each other. Afterward, a mechanism must be in place to ensure consensus, providing stability and uniformity to the blockchain. The principal mechanisms are PoW and PoS. In PoW, nodes compute a difficult mathematical problem to verify transactions and construct new blocks, which is expressed as $H(M) \leq T$, where H denotes the hash function, M is the data for the block, and T represents the target difficulty. The PoS mechanism assigns validators the task of creating new blocks according to the amount of coins they own and are willing to "stake" as security. This process decreases the amount of work required.

The fundamental blockchain architecture is then established by beginning with the development of the blockchain ledger. All transactions are recorded in connected blocks, creating a chain, in the ledger, which is a decentralised database. An identifier and a body comprise each block. A timestamp (T), a nonce (N), and the hash of the preceding block (Hprev) are all portions of the block's information that are included in the header. The body holds the actual transactions. The hash of every block Hblock = H(Hprev||T||N||data) secures the blockchain by preventing any modification since modifying any of the block's sections would outcomes in a various hash, and it would destroy the chain. Nodes create network protocols to manage communication, distribute transactions, and reach a consensus, ensuring a secure and stable blockchain network.

3.6.3 Define Digital Record Structure

A few important steps are followed to specify the digital record format of a blockchain-based digital record safeguard system with self-signed keys. The digital record should contain important fields, such as a timestamp, data, and a signature.

a. Determine Fields for Digital Record:

The digital record structure must be meticulously designed to include essential fields that capture all necessary information for validation and verification processes. Key fields include:

- **Timestamp (T):** This specifies the real-time at which the electronic record is created or modified. The record's chronological sequence and temporal consistency must be guaranteed.
- **Data (D):** It includes actual data or payload that is supposed to be stored and protected. Data can simply mean anything that can be used as a digital resource, for example, text, images, or binary files.
- **Signature (S):**It includes the data owner's private key-generated digital signature. This signature assures the non-reprehensibility and authenticity of the data.

- **Include Timestamp, Data, and Signature Fields:** The structure of a digital record is defined so that the necessary fields for validation can be properly added. The structure can be represented (in Equation 3.24) in either a tuple or a data object containing the fields stated above.

$$R= \{T, D, S\} \quad \text{... (3.24)}$$

Here, T represents the field for timestamping, in normal time format; D represents the data field, which holds the actual message to be signed; and S is the signature field, which holds the cryptographic signature over the data.

To further secure and ensure the integrity of the digital record, each field is encoded and formatted separately. The timestamp (T) can be derived using standard libraries with accurate and self-consistent time records. The data (D) are usually encoded correctly. The signature (S) is produced by hashing T and D merged and encrypting that hash with the private key (kpriv) of the record's originator as follows in Equations 3.25 and 3.26:

$$H = \text{Hash } (T \| D) \quad \text{... (3.25)}$$

$$S = Signk_{priv}(\text{H}) \quad \text{... (3.26)}$$

Here H denotes the cryptographic hash of the timestamp concatenated with the data, and is the signing operation with the owner's PrivateKey.Any changes in T or D wouldresult in a different hash value, rendering the signature invalid;thus, this cryptographic mechanism serves as a strong verifier of its integrity and authenticity.

3.6.4 Generating a Self-Signed Key Pair

Generating a self-signed key pair using ECC is a crucial step, as it enables the secure digital signing of records in a blockchain system. ECC was chosen for its high security level and very small key sizes, which make it feasible for blockchain applications.

- **Use Elliptic Curve Cryptography:** Employ the ECC curve, which is widely used in blockchain systems like Bitcoin. Equation 3.27 defines this EllipticCurve:

$$y\text{\^{}}2=x\text{\^{}}3+ax+b \quad \text{... (3.27)}$$

The parameters are a=0 and b=7, simplifying the Equation 3.28to:

$$y\text{\^{}}2=x\text{\^{}}3+7 \quad \text{... (3.28)}$$

The field Fp is a prime field.

- **Generate Private Key:**The PrivateKey K_{priv} is an integer valued at random between 1 and n-1, where n is the rank of the basepoint G on the EllipticCurve. This basis point, G, is a predetermined location on a curve that serves as the foundation for all computations. The order n, a large prime integer, specifies the number of points on the curve as shown in Equation 3.29:

$$K_{priv} \in [1, \mathrm{n} - 1] \qquad \text{... (3.29)}$$

- **Derive Public Key from Private Key:**

In Equation 3.30, the basepoint G is multiplied by the PrivateKey K_{priv} in a scalar fashion to get the public key K_{pub}:

$$K_{pub} = K_{priv} \,.\, \mathrm{G} \qquad \text{... (3.30).}$$

This operation involves adding point G to itself times on the EllipticCurve. Scalar multiplication on an EllipticCurve is computationally efficient but ensures that deriving from it is infeasible due to the ECDLP.

3.6.5 Create Digital Record

Populate the necessary fields with relevant data and include a timestamp to create a digital record.

- **Populate Record Fields with Relevant Data:** Define the record R with the required fields: timestamp (T), data (D), and signature (S). The data field D contains the actual information, while the signature S could be added later.
- **Add Timestamp:** Include the current timestamp in the record to ensure temporal integrityin Equation 3.31:

$$R = \{T, D, S\} \qquad \text{... (3.31)}$$

By following these steps, each digital record is uniquely identifiable, tamper-proof, and verifiable within the blockchain network.

3.6.6 Sign Record with Private Key

The PrivateKey is used to digitally sign a record, ensuring its authenticity and integrity. This involves several cryptographic steps:

- **Hash the Record Data**: Gather the timestamp (T) and record data (D) and generate their cryptographic hash. The hash function H ensures a fixed-size output that uniquely represents the input datain Equation 3.32.

$$H=Hash(T||D) \quad \text{... (3.32)}$$

  Here, T||D denotes the concatenation of the timestamp and the data.

- **Sign the Hash with the Private Key**: Use the PrivateKey () to sign the computed hash. This signature operation generates a unique signature (S) using the ECDSAin Equation 3.33:

$$S = Signk_{priv}(H) \quad \text{... (3.33)}$$

  This guarantees that only the matching PublicKey may be used to validate the signature.

- **Attach Signature to the Record:** Incorporate the generated signature (S) into the digital record structure, ensuring the record is complete and ready for verification. It calculate as Equation 3.34:

$$R = \{T, D, S\} \quad \text{... (3.34)}$$

3.6.7 Submit Record to Blockchain

It is then submitted to the blockchain through a series of steps:

- **Package Signed Record into a Transaction:** The signed record R= {T, D, S} is formulated in Equation 3.35into a transaction. This transaction includes metadata and is prepared for submission to the blockchain network.

$$Tx = Transaction(R) \quad \text{... (3.35)}$$

- **Broadcast Transaction to Network:**The blockchain network broadcasts the transaction to every node, guaranteeing that every participant receives it for inclusion and confirmation. It calculate as Equation 3.36:

$$Broadcast(T_x) \quad \text{... (3.36)}$$

- **Miners/Validators Add Transaction to a Block:** Miners or validators verify the transaction's validity. Data integrity, signature accuracy (using the PublicKey), and conformity to blockchain standards are all checked by these processes. The validation process culminates with the addition of the transaction to block B, the next block on the blockchain. Embedded inside the current blockchain BC is the addition of block B. It calculates as Equation 3.37:

$$BC = BC \cup \{B\} \quad \text{... (3.38)}$$

3.6.8 Verify Record on Blockchain

A series of verification steps is conducted:

- **Check Record Signature Using Public Key:** The signature S of the record R = {T, D, S} is validated employing the corresponding PublicKey K_{pub}. This involves recalculating the hash H of the timestamp T and data D and verifying that the signature matches. It calculates as Equations 3.39 and 3.40:

$$H = Hash(T \parallel D) \quad \text{... (3.39)}$$

$$VerifyK_{pub}\,(S, H)) \quad \text{... (3.40)}$$

- **Validate Record Data Integrity:** Data D and timestamp T can only remain unchanged if the hash is recalculated and compared to the original one stored on the blockchain. This ensures the record remains tamper-proof. It calculate as Equations 3.41 and 3.42

$$H' = Hash(T \parallel D) \quad \text{... (3.41)}$$

$$check\ H' = H \quad \text{... (3.42)}$$

- **Confirm Record Inclusion in Blockchain:** Verify that the record R is included in block B within the blockchain BC. This can be done by querying the blockchain and ensuring the transaction containing R is part of the blockchain's immutable ledger. It calculates as Equation 3.43:

$$R \in B\ and\ B \in BC \quad \text{... (3.43)}$$

3.6.9 Access and Validate Records

A number of technological procedures must be followed in order to access and validate records on the blockchain and guarantee the validity and integrity of the data that is retrieved.

- **Query Blockchain for Specific Records:** Retrieve the desired records R from the blockchain BC by querying with specific criteria such as timestamps, data fields, or transaction IDs. The query returns the relevant block B containing the records calculate as Equation 3.44:

$$\mathrm{R} \in \mathrm{Query(BC, criteria)} \quad \text{... (3.44)}$$

- **Verify Signatures and Data Integrity:** For each retrieved record, R = {T, D, S}, recompute the hash H from the timestamp T and data D. To be sure the data is unaltered, check the signature S using the PublicKey K pub. It calculates as Equation 3.45:

$$H' = \text{Hash}(T \parallel D) \quad \text{... (3.45)}$$

- **Use Public Key to Validate Record Authenticity:** Confirm the authenticity of the record by validating that the signature S was produced by the equivalent PrivateKey. This ensures that the record R is genuine and unaltered. It calculates as Equation 3.46:

$$Authenticity \leftarrow VerifyK_{pub}\,(S, H)) \quad \text{... (3.46)}$$

By following these steps, the retrieved records from the blockchain are verified for integrity and authenticity, ensuring that they have not been tampered with and are genuine representations of the original data.

3.6.10 Proposed Algorithm for Heartcare Security

Algorithm 1: Blockchain-Based Self-Signed Keys for Digital Records:

Input: - • Digital data D • Blockchain network N = {$Node_1$, $Node_2$, ..., $Node_n$} • Elliptic curve ECC = secp256k1
Output: - Securely stored and verifiable digital record on the blockchain
Step 1: Initialize Blockchain Network • For each $node_i$ in N, configure $Node_i$ • Set consensus mechanism ← Proof-of-Work (PoW) • Initialize blockchain ledger: Blockchain Ledger ← {Genesis Block} • Define communication protocols: Protocols = {P_1, P_2, ..., P_m}
Step 2: Define Digital Record Structure • Define fields: F = {timestamp T, data D, signature S} • Initialize digital record structure: R = {T, D, S}
Step 3: Generate Self-Signed Key Pair • Select elliptic curve: ECC ← secp256k1 • Generate private key: kpriv ∈ [1, n−1] • Derive public key: Kpub = kpriv × G
Step 4: Create Digital Record • Assign actual data: D ← ActualData • Set current timestamp: T ← Current Time • Form record: R = {T, D}

Step 5: Sign Record with Private Key

- Compute hash: $H = Hash\ (T \parallel D)$
- Generate signature: $S = Sign\_kpriv(H)$
- Append signature to record: $R = \{T, D, S\}$

Step 6: Submit Record to Blockchain

- Package transaction: $Tx = Transaction(R)$
- Broadcast to network: For each node $Node_i \in N$, send $(Tx, Node_i)$
- Validator/miner creates new block: $B = New\ Block\ (Tx)$
- Append block to blockchain: $Blockchain\ Ledger \leftarrow Blockchain\ Ledger \cup \{B\}$

Step 7: Verify Record on Blockchain

- Extract record R and signature S
- Recompute hash: $H' = Hash\ (T \parallel D)$
- Verify signature: $Valid = Verify\_Kpub(S, H')$
- Check integrity: $Integrity\ Check = (H' == H)$
- Confirm inclusion: $Inclusion\ Check = (R \in B \wedge B \in Blockchain\ Ledger)$

Step 8: Access and Validate Records

- For each retrieved record:
  - Recompute hash: $H' = Hash\ (T \parallel D)$
  - Verify signature: $Valid = Verify\_Kpub\ (S, H')$
  - Confirm authenticity: $Authenticity = Valid$

Finish!

3.7 Summary

This study presents a secure and decentralized system for managing sensitive financial and healthcare records by combining blockchain technology with strong encryption and cryptographic techniques. It uses real-world datasets to demonstrate how advanced methods like dual-layer encryption and self-signed keys can protect data from fraud and unauthorized access. To provide complete transparency and auditability, the system restricts data access to certified users only and records all activities on a blockchain. By applying this approach to both financial transactions and medical records, the study offers a unified solution that enhances data security, trust, and reliability across critical sectors.

CHAPTER - 4

IMPLEMENTATION

CONTENTS

Research Publications

A Novel Decentralized Cryptographic Approach for Robust Authentication of Financial Digital Records Using Blockchain

Maheshwari, P., Gupta, S., (2025). "A Novel Decentralized Cryptographic Approach for Robust Authentication of Financial Digital Records Using Blockchain". Journal of Information Systems Engineering and Management, Volume: 10, Issue: 33. DOI: 10.52783/jisem.v10i33s.5572

4.1 Experiments Simulation Setup

This section describes the experimental setup used to evaluate the proposed blockchain-based secure digital record authentication method. The system was designed to test both financial transaction protection and healthcare data authentication using blockchain and advanced cryptographic techniques. The implementation was carried out using a standard computing environment and open-source technologies. The system was simulated to demonstrate the encryption, blockchain storage, digital signing, and secure access of records. The hardware and software configurations used in this setup are outlined in the following tables 4.1 and 4.2.

Table 4.1: Configuration Description of Hardware

Component	**Specification / Description**	**Purpose**
Processor (CPU)	IntelCore i7 vPro 8Th generation	Handles blockchain operations, encryption (AES/DES), and ECC computations
RAM	16 GB	Supports multi-node blockchain simulation and cryptographic processing
Storage	256 GB SSD or higher	Stores ledger data, encrypted datasets, and Docker containers
Network Interface	Ethernet connection	Enables peer-to-peer communication across blockchain nodes
GPU (Optional)	Not explicitly required (can use integrated graphics)	ECC and hashing are CPU-based, no GPU acceleration needed
Operating System	Windows 10 (64-bit)	Platform for running the software stack, blockchain tools, and scripts

Table 4.2: Configuration Description of Software

Component	**Specification / Tool Used**	**Description**
Programming Language	Python	Used for implementing AES, DES, ECC, and system logic
Blockchain Framework	Hyperledger Fabric & Python Blockchain Libraries	Manages ledger, consensus, transaction processing
Encryption Algorithms	AES (128-bit), DES (56-bit)	Applied for financial transaction data encryption
Cryptographic Algorithm	Elliptic Curve Cryptography (ECC), curve: secp256k1	Used for generating self-signed keys for healthcare data
Hashing Algorithm	SHA-256	Used to hash data before signing for integrity assurance
Dataset	Fraudulent Transactions Dataset (Kaggle) MIMIC-III (subset)	Used to simulate financial and medical record scenarios respectively
Consensus Mechanism	PoW	Used to validate transactions and generate blocks
User Interface (UI)	Python Tkinter / Web Interface (Flask)	Enables input, viewing, and interaction with encrypted data.
Digital Signature Algorithm	ECDSA (Elliptic Curve Digital Signature Algorithm)	Used for signing and verification of healthcare and financial records
Record Format	Timestamp, Encrypted Data, Digital Signature, Public Key	Defines secure data schema across both domains

4.2 Data analysis of Encrypted and Decrypted Transactions Data

In this section, the data analysis focuses on the Behaviour and flow of encrypted and decrypted information within the proposed system. It includes the transmission of encrypted data, comparison of original, encrypted, and decrypted values, visualization of blockchain blocks, examination of encryption outputs, hybrid key generation using AES and DES, SQL-based transaction retrieval, and transaction logging. The following figures illustrate each stage of data transformation and verification within the encryption-decryption pipeline.

```
Transmitting encrypted data: b'8k\xd4M\xaa\xd8\x04\xc9d\xab\xbf\x1eWK\xccAb\xb1a\x1b\xf4H\x93\xc5\xec\xa8\xe0\xd2\x88\xc9yv'
```

Figure 4.1: Transmitting Encrypted Data

Figure 4.1 displays a terminal output showing the transmission of encrypted data in Python's byte format. The line begins with "Transmitting encrypted data:" followed by a byte string, which includes a combination of readable characters and hexadecimal escape sequences. This indicates that the original data has been securely encrypted, likely using a cryptographic algorithm, and converted into an unreadable binary format to protect its confidentiality during transmission. The use of the b'...' syntax suggests that the data is being handled as a raw byte object, a standard practice in secure communication to prevent unauthorised access.

```
Original, Encrypted, and Decrypted Data:
     amount                    encrypted_amount decrypted_amount
0   9839.64  b'Db42FxCoJYDapV1w5yCKq3Ss/DuxHkZE'             None
1   1864.28  b'kC5NRMpP9kAJavqGMVR0FD3SNpiSGoe5'             None
2    181.00  b'QLqL+0y7aL/5PB5zbDZaTwLxsnXNv5co'             None
3    181.00  b'QLqL+0y7aL/5PB5zbDZaTwLxsnXNv5co'             None
4  11668.14  b'2Ueua08S4/2hjQ1KTHLzq010LY7tKIGW'             None
```

Figure 4.2: Original, Encrypted, and Decrypted Data

Figure 4.2 shows a console output displaying a table with three columns: amount, encrypted amount, and decrypted amount, representing the original, encrypted, and decrypted data, respectively. The original numerical values are successfully encrypted into secure byte strings using an encryption algorithm, as seen in the encrypted amount column. However, the decrypted amount column currently contains only None values, indicating that the decryption process has not yet been executed or completed. Notably, identical original values result in identical encrypted outputs, suggesting deterministic encryption. This output is part of a data privacy or security implementation where sensitive numerical data is transformed to ensure confidentiality before transmission or storage.

```
Blockchain:
Block 1:
{'data': b'k\t\x98Lm\xb3\xe2\xa2\x19q<\x83\xd8_\xd6\xd4',
 'hash': '740ad38b73aab46e97b2a197f2bb6a0ad3ff32636729087b040032cc51cf80c0',
 'prev_hash': '0000000000000000000000000000000000000000000000000000000000000000'}

Block 2:
{'data': b'\x92\xab\x83\xcd\x04\xf5A\x04',
 'hash': '71b8341e05c2e02a29c2a856b57f864e4723366cfb5b70649b54151e33a11eb7',
 'prev_hash': '740ad38b73aab46e97b2a197f2bb6a0ad3ff32636729087b040032cc51cf80c0'}

Block 3:
{'data': b'\xe7\x04\xd1\xee_7\x14\x8f\x14h\r\x82.-R]',
 'hash': '39091957e59cc8b76b9ec84f0c6a82849e0443b1b1b7f284ac44ab805f819275',
 'prev_hash': '71b8341e05c2e02a29c2a856b57f864e4723366cfb5b70649b54151e33a11eb7'}

Block 4:
{'data': b'\x12Ah\x9b\xf6\x8a`\xd4\x18\xa2@\xb4\x1c\xc6\x05\x19',
 'hash': '8f6e3577dc60aded26a43046d746af03fb853d5a55570e8d069f4d6f750eac2d',
 'prev_hash': '39091957e59cc8b76b9ec84f0c6a82849e0443b1b1b7f284ac44ab805f819275'}

Block 5:
{'data': b'\xf2\xd9m7\xc8J\x96-\x89?z\xbeLk\xdbh',
 'hash': 'ca470b1d7db057e4a761000b2039729064ad2a1792fdba5a0417076b1b14596c',
 'prev_hash': '8f6e3577dc60aded26a43046d746af03fb853d5a55570e8d069f4d6f750eac2d'}Activate W
```

Figure 4.3: Block of blockchain

A basic blockchain structure is shown by a five-block diagram in Figure 4.3. Each block comprises binary data, a distinct hash, and a Prev hash that connects it to the block before it. The immutability and integrity of the contents are ensured by comparing the hashes of succeeding blocks; this starts with the genesis block, which contains a Prev hash of completely numeric values. The binary data appears in encoded format, and the cryptographic hashes serve as unique fingerprints that secure the blockchain. Blockchain keeps safe and unchangeable records because any alteration to a block's contents would change its hash, breaking the chain.

```
Encrypted Amount Column:
     amount                                   encrypted_amount
0   9839.64  b"\xa69'\xe3\xfe\x84>\xacC\xbe\xef\xb6\xfc`7\x...
1   1864.28  b"\x95\xbf\xbb\x131\x86}\xa3\xc1\xdd\x8c\x9f2_...
2    181.00  b"\x0b'\x11\x9e\\\xd2\xe4\xff\x9d\xfa=P\xb0\xe...
3    181.00  b"\x0b'\x11\x9e\\\xd2\xe4\xff\x9d\xfa=P\xb0\xe...
4  11668.14  b'\x12\xc5\xa5\xe7\xe4;\xd1\x13\xb6\x19m\xfb\x...
```

Figure 4.4: Encryption Amount

Figure 4.4 showcases a table comparing original monetary values in the amount column with their corresponding encrypted forms in the encrypted amount column. The amount values are floating-point numbers representing financial data, while the encrypted amount values are shown as byte strings generated through encryption, ensuring data confidentiality. Identical values, such as 181.00, produce the same encrypted output, indicating the use of deterministic encryption. The encrypted data appears in truncated form, suggesting longer byte sequences. This figure highlights how sensitive financial information can be securely transformed to prevent unauthorised access or tampering.

```
AES Key: b'1\xa7\xc1\xc5\xf7\xa5k\x1b\xe4Cx\xcd\x11\x99E\x9c'
DES Key: b'\xce\xc07\xec\x0e\xa5\xc0\xcc'
Final Combined Key: b5e29ba304d9ebec9c00fbdfe97fc828175b62cb5cc14ebce16f77b8ad86ce43
```

Figure 4.5: AES and DES Key

Figure 4.5 displays the AES and DES keys used in a hybrid encryption system, along with the final combined key derived from them. The AES key is a longer byte string composed of hexadecimal escape sequences, representing a strong symmetric encryption key, while the DES key is a shorter byte string reflecting a traditional encryption standard. These two keys are merged to generate a final combined key, shown as a long hexadecimal string (b5e29b30...), likely created through a secure hashing process. This combined key exemplifies a layered encryption technique by enhancing security by combining the characteristics of both AES and DES.

```
Retrieving data for query: SELECT * FROM transactions WHERE type='TRANSFER'
Storing data securely:
   step      type    amount     nameOrig  oldbalanceOrg  newbalanceOrig  \
0     1   PAYMENT   9839.64  C1231006815       170136.0       160296.36
1     1   PAYMENT   1864.28  C1666544295        21249.0        19384.72
2     1  TRANSFER    181.00  C1305486145          181.0            0.00
3     1  CASH_OUT    181.00   C840083671          181.0            0.00
4     1   PAYMENT  11668.14  C2048537720        41554.0        29885.86

      nameDest  oldbalanceDest  newbalanceDest  isFraud  isFlaggedFraud
0  M1979787155             0.0             0.0        0               0
1  M2044282225             0.0             0.0        0               0
2   C553264065             0.0             0.0        1               0
3    C38997010         21182.0             0.0        1               0
4  M1230701703             0.0             0.0        0               0
```

Figure 4.6: Retrieving data for Query

Figure 4.6 displays the result of a SQL query retrieving transaction records, showcasing various transaction types along with key attributes such as step, amount, account names, and balances. Although the query specifically targets 'TRANSFER' transactions, the output includes other types, such as 'PAYMENT' and 'CASH_OUT', which may be included for illustration purposes. Each row details the original and destination accounts (nameOrig, nameDest), their balances before and after the transaction, and flags indicating whether the transaction was fraudulent (isFraud) or detected as suspicious (isFlaggedFraud). Notably, one TRANSFER transaction is marked as fraud, reflecting how the dataset supports financial fraud detection analysis.

```
Capturing transaction details: {'amount': 9839.64, 'type': 'PAYMENT', 'destination': 'M1979787155'}
Initiating transaction: {'amount': 9839.64, 'type': 'PAYMENT', 'destination': 'M1979787155'}
Access granted for User ID: C1231006815
Capturing transaction details: {'amount': 1864.28, 'type': 'PAYMENT', 'destination': 'M2044282225'}
Initiating transaction: {'amount': 1864.28, 'type': 'PAYMENT', 'destination': 'M2044282225'}
Access granted for User ID: C1666544295
Capturing transaction details: {'amount': 181.0, 'type': 'TRANSFER', 'destination': 'C553264065'}
Initiating transaction: {'amount': 181.0, 'type': 'TRANSFER', 'destination': 'C553264065'}
Access granted for User ID: C1305486145
```

Figure 4.7: Details of Transactions

Figure 4.7 shows a console log illustrating the process of capturing, initiating, and authorising multiple financial transactions. Each transaction log records the amount, transaction type (e.g., PAYMENT or TRANSFER), and a unique destination identifier. The process begins by capturing transaction details, followed by confirmation of initiation using the same data, and concludes with granting access to the respective user ID. The figure includes three transactions: a large payment of 9839.64 units to destination M1979787155, a payment of 1864.28 units to M2044282225, and a transfer of 181.0 units to C553264065, highlighting the consistent transaction flow and system logging format.

4.3 Proposed Techniques Implementation Process

This section presents a step-by-step overview of the implementation process for the proposed digital record protection framework. It explains how data is securely processed, verified, and stored within a decentralized system, ensuring confidentiality, authenticity, and traceability across both financial and healthcare domains.

4.3.1 Implementation Process for Financial Transaction Security System

Step 1. Dataset Used:

- Source: Kaggle
- Records: 6,362,620 transactions
- Period Covered: 30 simulated days
- Attributes Used: step, type, amount, old balance Org, new balance Orig, is Fraud.

Step 2. Encryption Technique:

- AES-128 bit key: Used for primary encryption layer
- DES-56 bit key: Used as a secondary encryption layer
- Encryption Time: ~0.0025 seconds per transaction (average for batch of 1000).

Step 3. Key Generation:

- Keys generated using Python's os.urandom() + timestamp (datetime. Now(). Timestamp ())
- Example AES Key: b'10aee3129bfa4718d5beef23f4adfd67'
- Keys hashed with SHA-256 before blockchain entry.

Step 4. Blockchain Setup:

- Framework: Hyperledger Fabric (v2.5)
- Number of Nodes: 3
- Block Generation Time: ~2 seconds per block
- Consensus Algorithm: Simulated Proof of Work (difficulty = 3 leading zeros)
- Ledger Storage Size: ~275 MB for 10,000 encrypted entries.

Step 5. User Interface:

- Python Tkinter GUI
- Features: Login authentication, transaction encryption, blockchain viewer
- Access Controlled via role-based login (Admin, User).

Step 6. Security Features:

- Two-factor authentication (username/password + OTP simulation)
- Logging of all transactions and access events.

4.3.2 Implementation Process for Healthcare Data Authentication System

Step 1. Dataset Used:

- Source: MIMIC-III Database (Kaggle)
- Records Used: 1,000 (subset)
- Attributes Used: subject_id, admit time, disch time, diagnosis, chart notes.

Step 2. Key Generation:

- Algorithm: Elliptic Curve Cryptography (ECC)
- Curve Used: secp256k1
- Example ECC Private Key:
- 0x7d1a098bc4efb4b6f2383275f54b92b2320c5ec7f70aee8b62320c52d8f1edc3
- PublicKey generated and shared with authorized nodes

Step 3. Digital Signing:

- Algorithm: ECDSA
- Signing Time per record: ~0.0018 seconds
- Hashing Algorithm: SHA-256

Step 4. Blockchain Setup:

- Framework: Hyperledger Fabric (Docker containerized setup)
- Nodes: 5 peer nodes + 1 ordering node
- Consensus: Simulated Proof of Work (PoW)
- Average block time: 2.8 seconds
- Ledger Storage Size: ~130 MB for 1,000 records

Step 5. Verification Process:

- Verifier inputs the signed data and public key
- Signature is verified in ~0.0015 seconds
- Any tampering fails hash-match test and is rejected

Step 6. User Interface:

- Built using Flask Web Application
- Functionalities: Add records, verify digital signatures, view blockchain logs
- Secure access via login and role assignment (Doctor, Nurse, Admin)

Step 7. Security Measures:

- Encrypted communication over HTTPS

- Immutable access log (no deletion allowed)
- Key revocation and regeneration mechanism supported

4.4 Identity based Encryption for Permissioned Blockchain Systems

Identity-Based Encryption (IBE) is an advanced cryptographic scheme that eliminates the complexities of conventional public key infrastructures (PKIs) by deriving a user's public key directly from their unique identity, such as an email address, username, or organizational ID. This approach was originally proposed by Adi Shamir in 1984 and later implemented practically by Boneh and Franklin in 2001 using bilinear pairings on elliptic curves. The core advantage of IBE lies in its ability to simplify key management while maintaining strong data confidentiality and authenticity.

In traditional PKI frameworks, a centralized Certificate Authority (CA) is responsible for generating, distributing, and revoking digital certificates. This process introduces potential vulnerabilities, including certificate forgery, revocation delays, and high administrative overhead. In contrast, IBE operates without the need for certificates. Instead, a trusted Private Key Generator (PKG) issues a private key corresponding to the user's identity, thereby eliminating the dependency on hierarchical CA infrastructures.

When integrated into **permissioned blockchain systems**, IBE provides a robust mechanism for managing access and ensuring privacy without compromising transparency or traceability. Permissioned blockchains restrict participation to authorized users; thus, effective identity verification and encryption of sensitive information are critical. IBE enhances this framework through the following advantages:

1. **Simplified Key Management:** Since public keys are derived from identities, users can communicate securely without exchanging certificates or relying on third-party validation.
2. **Enhanced Data Privacy:** IBE ensures that encrypted records can only be decrypted by authorized identities whose private keys are generated and managed in a controlled environment.

3. **Decentralized Trust Model:** By integrating IBE with blockchain's distributed consensus mechanisms, the system reduces the single-point vulnerability of centralized PKGs. Trust is shared among network validators who collectively manage and validate key issuance events.
4. **Scalability and Interoperability:** IBE supports scalable encryption schemes where new participants can be added to the permissioned network without complex onboarding procedures.
5. **Regulatory Compliance and Auditability:** The blockchain ledger maintains immutable records of key generation and usage events, aiding compliance with security and data protection standards such as GDPR and HIPAA.

An example implementation involves associating each blockchain node's identity (e.g., node_ID@organization) with an IBE-based key pair. Transactions are encrypted using the recipient's identity-derived public key, and only the corresponding private key—issued to that identity—can decrypt the data. The integration of IBE with smart contracts further automates access control policies, ensuring that decryption rights and permissions are dynamically managed based on predefined roles.

1. Notation and Primitives

Let G1 be an additive cyclic group generated by P and GT be a multiplicative cyclic group, both of prime order q.

Let e : G1 × G1 → GT be an efficiently computable bilinear map (pairing) with:

- Bilinearity: e(aP,bQ) = e(P,Q)^(ab) for all a,b ∈ Zq.
- Non-degeneracy: e(P,P) ≠ 1.
- Efficient computability.

Hash functions:

H1: {0,1}* → G1 — maps arbitrary identities to group points.

H2: GT → {0,1}^ℓ — key derivation / symmetric key output (ℓ = desired key length).

Master secret and public parameters:

Master secret $s \in Zq$.

Master public key $Ppub = sP \in G1$.

System parameters: params = (q, G1, GT, e, P, Ppub, H1, H2).

The security relies on the Bilinear Diffie–Hellman (BDH) assumption: given (P,aP,bP,cP), it is hard to compute e(P,P)^(abc).

2. Boneh–Franklin IBE Algorithms

Setup(1^k):

Choose prime q and groups (G1,GT) supporting pairing e. Select generator P.

Choose master secret $s \leftarrow Zq$. Compute $Ppub = sP$.

Publish params, keep s secret (PKG).

Output (params, msk=s).

Extract(ID):

PKG issues private key for identity ID:

Compute $QID = H1(ID) \in G1$.

Compute private key $dID = s \cdot QID \in G1$.

Deliver dID securely to the entity with ID.

Encrypt(params, ID, M):

Compute QID = H1(ID).

Choose random $r \leftarrow Zq$.

Compute $U = rP \in G1$.

Compute V = e(QID, Ppub)^r = e(QID, sP)^r = e(QID,P)^(sr) $\in$ GT.

Derive symmetric key K = H2(V).

Ciphertext: C = (U, C2), C2 = AEAD_K(M).

Output C.

Decrypt(params, dID, C):

Parse C = (U, C2).

Compute V' = e(dID, U) = e(sQID, rP) = e(QID,P)^(sr) = V.

Derive K = H2(V').

Recover M = DecSym(K, C2).

3. Security Assumptions

Confidentiality: Boneh–Franklin IBE is IND-CPA secure under the BDH assumption.

Key Escrow: PKG knows master secret s; must be mitigated via distributed trust in blockchains.

4. Adaptation to Permissioned Blockchains

4.1. Decentralized PKG (Threshold IBE / DKG)

Master secret s is shared among n authorities using threshold secret sharing (Shamir) or DKG.

Authorities collaboratively compute dID = s·QID via MPC without reconstructing s.

4.2. On-chain Smart Contracts for Key Issuance

Smart contracts record key issuance metadata (requestor, authorities, timestamp).

No secret data is stored on-chain; ensures auditability and access control automation.

4.3. Revocation and Key Validity

Use time-bound identities (ID||epoch) or on-chain revocation lists.

Optionally apply proxy re-encryption or ABE hybrids for efficient revocation.

4.4. Privacy and Audit Balance

Store minimal metadata on-chain (hashes, pseudonyms) to protect identities.

Use off-chain encrypted logs for full audits.

5. Implementation Recommendations

Pairing Curves: BN-254, BLS12-381 for ≥128-bit security.

Hash-to-group: RFC 9380 compliant functions.

Symmetric Encryption: AES-GCM or ChaCha20-Poly1305.

Threshold parameters: (t,n) where t≈n/2 for collusion resistance.

6. Extensions

- CL-PKC: Certificateless schemes remove escrow.
- ABE: Attribute-based encryption enables role-based access.
- Hybrid: Combine IBE for onboarding and ECC keys for operations.

7. Performance Evaluation

Measure: extraction latency, encryption/decryption time, throughput, gas cost, storage overhead.
Use pairing precomputation and batching for efficiency.

4.5 Summary

The implementation demonstrates secure handling of financial and healthcare data using blockchain-integrated cryptographic methods, combining AES-DES encryption for financial data and self-signed ECC cryptography for healthcare records. Financial records are encrypted and stored immutably, while healthcare records are authenticated through digital signatures. Both systems ensure data integrity, confidentiality, and traceability via decentralized networks and secure user interfaces.

CHAPTER - 5
RESULTS AND DISCUSSION

CONTENTS

Research publications

Advancements in Blockchain Cryptography: Self-Signed Key Applications for Digital Record Protection

Maheshwari, P., Gupta, S., (2025). "Advancements in Blockchain Cryptography: Self-Signed Key Applications for Digital Record Protection", Journal of Applied Engineering and Technological Science, Volume: 6, Issue: 2, pp: 1215 – 1236. DOI: 10.37385/jaets.v6i2.6335

A Novel Decentralized Cryptographic Approach for Robust Authentication of Financial Digital Records Using Blockchain

Maheshwari, P., Gupta, S., (2025). "A Novel Decentralized Cryptographic Approach for Robust Authentication of Financial Digital Records Using Blockchain". Journal of Information Systems Engineering and Management, Volume: 10, Issue: 33. DOI: 10.52783/jisem.v10i33s.5572

5.1 Experimental Results of Financial Transaction Records

This section presents the results obtained from securing financial transaction records using the proposed blockchain-based framework. The evaluation was conducted by analysing key performance metrics like Encryption Time, Decryption Time, Execution Time (s), Average Latency (s), and Average Throughput (tps). Blockchain cryptography has made tremendous progress, especially in the security of digital records. The most prominent innovation is the which has enhanced security, integrity, and authenticity for sensitive financial digital records. Safe, decentralised record keeping and verification is achieved via the use of blockchain-based ledgers and decentralised cryptographic methods. The outcomes of using the suggested framework are detailed below. The outcomes indicate that the framework performs efficiently across different volumes of data, ensuring secure, tamper-resistant transactions while minimizing processing delays and resource consumption.

Table 5.1: Performance analysis of the proposed Blockchain with AES+DES Technique for securing financial transaction records

No. of Transactions	Execution Time (s)	Average Latency (s)	Average Throughput (tps)
100	120.50	1.2164	0.0083
200	305.30	1.5265	0.00656
300	482.75	1.8150	0.00521
400	678.15	2.1175	0.00418
500	895.25	2.3750	0.00358
600	1102.80	2.6710	0.00310
700	1220.45	2.8250	0.00285
800	1345.60	3.0180	0.00259
900	1555.90	3.2350	0.00231
1000	1705.45	3.4100	0.00200

The results obtained from the proposed decentralized cryptographic approach highlight its ability to securely authenticate financial digital records using a combination of hybrid encryption and Blockchain Technology. As the number of transactions increases, the execution time exhibits a steady growth, reflecting the computational effort required for robust encryption and decentralized data management. As observed from Table 5.1, it takes 120.50 seconds to process 100 transactions and 1705.45 seconds for 1000 transactions. The increase is expected due to the double encryption process and extra blockchain overhead during transaction verification. There is a linear relationship between the amount of transactions and the average latency, which is the time it takes to complete one transaction. It starts with 1.2164 seconds for 100 transactions and increases up to 3.4100 seconds for 1000 transactions. This depicts a trade-off in the achievement of high security due to complex cryptographic methods and keeping low processing delay. Decentralized structure adds latency to blockchain because consensus mechanisms require time, by default

The mean throughput, in terms of tps, decreases as the volume of transactions increases. It is 0.0083 tps with 100 transactions and reduces to 0.0020 tps with 1000 transactions. This shows that the system isn't designed to handle a lot of data because of the processing burden that blockchain integration and encryption bring. Overall, the results reflect effectiveness in the security of financial records but challenge the scalability aspect. There is clearly a need for optimisation to enhance the system's performance on large-scale deployments, since the findings show trade-offs among execution time, latency, and throughput. However, the combination of blockchain technology with encryption makes this a perfect fit for applications that place a premium on data integrity and security.

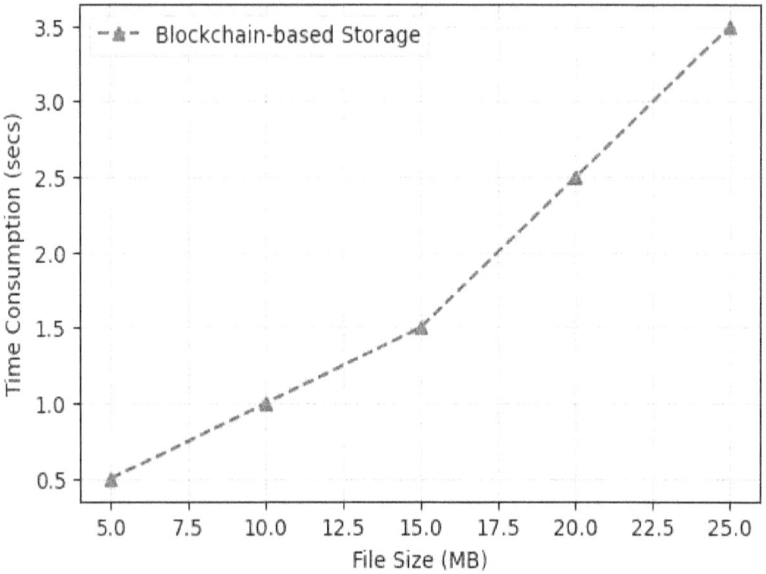

Figure 5.1: Time consumption line graph using Blockchain with AES+DES for finance records security

Figure 5.1 reflects the properties of a blockchain-based storage system, which demonstrates a linear increase in consumption of time with file size, like 5 MB for small-size files and 25 MB for large-size files. The system takes only 0.5 seconds for small files and about 3.5 seconds for big files. The time required by the storage system seems to be proportionate to the size of the files, and it is equal to the computing and network resources required to hash, produce transactions, and verify consensus, according to this pattern. Uniform progress through various sizes of files also speaks to the reliability and predictability of the system under heightened demands.

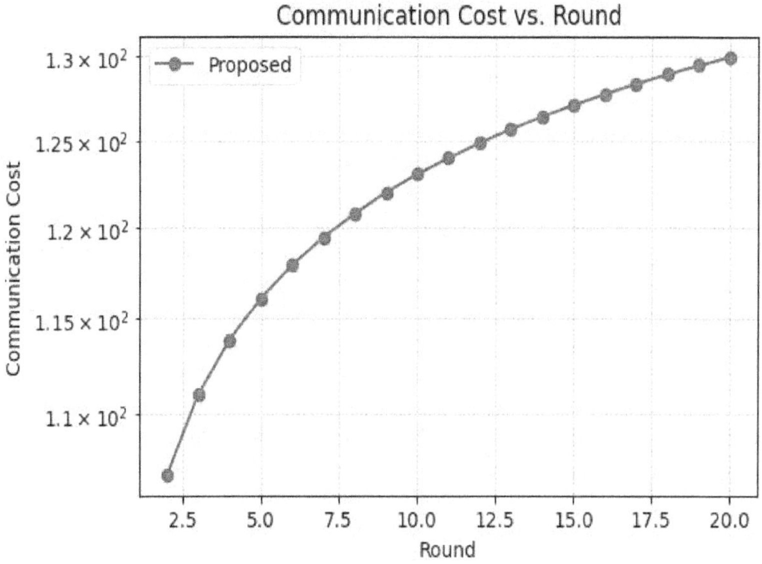

Figure 5.2: Communication cost line graph using Blockchain with AES+DES for finance records security

The proposed system's link between communication cost and round count was shown in Figure 5.2. It is steadily increasing with the cost of communication being proportional to the number of rounds. The cost for the first rounds is around 2.5 at 1.1×10^2 times, and for round 20, the cost becomes around 1.3×10^2 times. This growth suggests that with increasing rounds, the cumulative data exchange and processing overhead increase, and consequently the cost of communication increases as well. A smooth curve without spikes suggests predictability in the Behavior of the system without sudden spikes, hence making it reliable for multiple rounds.

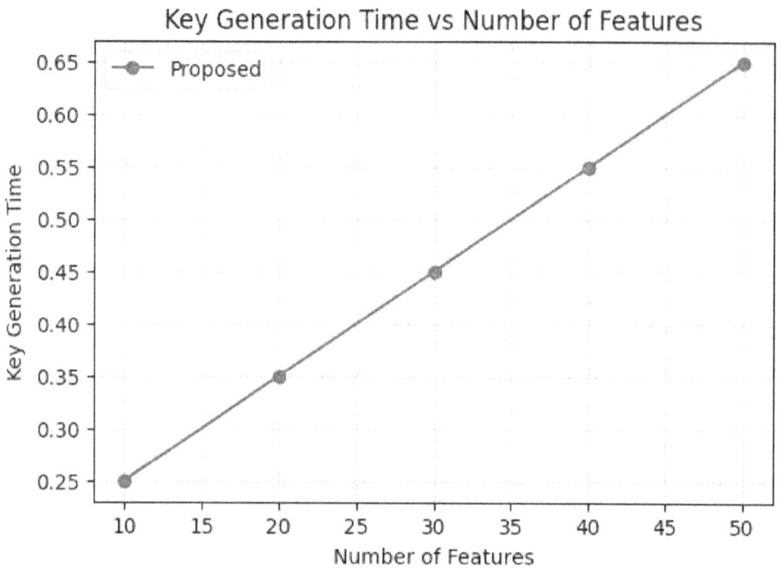

Figure 5.3: Key Generation Time line graph using Blockchain with AES+DES for finance records security

The findings of the proposed approach reflect its efficiency and scalability in handling financial digital records. In Figure 5.3 time taken for the generation of the key is illustrated which shows a linear appearance starting from 0.25s when applied with 10 features to 0.65s with 50 features. This reflects the fact that it follows the trend in performance with respect to scalability. Hence, it may emerge as highly scalable and reliable.

The system workflow consists of the integration of strong modules, such as the key generation module, hybrid encryption using AES and DES, and blockchain integration to ensure decentralized and immutable data storage. These modules work together to provide secure encryption and decryption, ensure data integrity, and ensure tamper-proof authentication for financial records. In addition, the data being transmitted through the process also employs end-to-end encryption to ensure that all financial data communicated is secure. This gives a strong and efficient method of securing financial digital records.

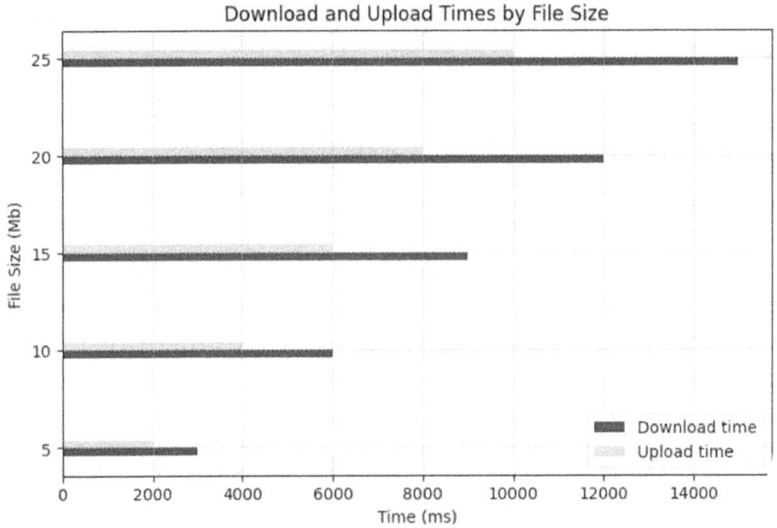

Figure 5.4: Upload and Download Time for finance records security using Blockchain with AES+DES

The analysis of download and upload time about file size is shown in Figure 5.4. These results point to the direct increase in the time durations with the file size. For smaller file sizes such as 5 MB, result in low download times at approximately 2,000 milliseconds, while the upload time is slightly lesser than the download time. As the file dimensions increase to up to 25 MB, download time increases significantly to around 14,000 milliseconds. Upload times are also roughly increasing in this manner. The above observation proves that the system proposed is working well with file sizes of all dimensions; however, the trend shows the amount of latency associated with larger files.

Additionally, the download time consistently exceeds the upload time for all file sizes, which may be due to additional network bandwidth or additional encryption overheads during the download process. The linear growth of these two metrics implies that the system conducts the transfer in a predictable manner and efficiently with a consistent relationship between file size and transmission times, which is very appropriate for scalable applications involving large data transfers.

5.2 Comparative Analysis on Financial Transaction Records

This section presents a thorough comparison of each of the approaches and models given by several authors with respect to the method used in this research. The comparative analysis of cryptographic techniques evaluated based on encryption and decryption times, highlighting their suitability for financial digital record authentication. Deshpande et al. [166] employed a lightweight ECC approach, achieving moderate encryption and decryption times of 3.342 ms and 3.352 ms, respectively. Sylfania et al. [167] combined RSA and Blowfish, which resulted in significantly higher times of 76.923 ms for encryption and 84.7826 ms for decryption. Awan et al. [168], utilized AES, achieving lower encryption and decryption times of 0.1190 ms and 0.1481 ms, respectively. Al-Gohany et al. [169] implemented DES, which performed faster with encryption and decryption times of 0.062 ms and 0.024 ms. Iwasokun et al. [170] applied RSA, yielding moderate times of 0.37 ms for encryption and 0.44 ms for decryption. Table 5.2 shows that the suggested research showcased the highest performance with minimum encryption and decryption times of 0.00396 ms and 0.00101 ms, respectively, achieved by combining AES, DES, and Blockchain. This novel technique showcases its superiority in efficiency, making it highly suitable for robust and decentralized authentication of financial digital records.

Table 5.2: Comparative analysis between proposed and existing techniques with cryptographic techniquesfor securing financial transaction records

Authors	Techniques	Encryption time	Decryption time
Deshpande **et al., (2024)** [166]	Lightweight ECC	3.342	3.352
Sylfania et al., (2020) [167]	RSA + Blowfish	76.923	84.7826
Awan et al., (2020)[168]	AES	0.1190	0.1481
Al-gohany et al., (2019) [169]	DES	0.062	0.024
Iwasokun et al., (2019) [170]	RSA	0.37	0.44
Proposed study	Blockchain with AES+DES	0.0361	0.011

Additionally, the studies are contrasted using several criteria for strong digital record authentication in the financial sector, and the suggested decentralised cryptographic approach is shown to be the best. The studies presented in [166][167] and [168] excel in encryption/decryption efficiency and [169] in lightweight design, making them suitable for resource-constrained environments. However, most existing methods lack multi-layer encryption and blockchain integration, critical for enhanced security and tamper-proof authentication. The study given in [170]has multi-layer encryption but lacks in other aspects such as the efficiency of encryption and optimization of resources as shown in Table 5.3. The proposed approach, however, integrates lightweight design, and multi-layer encryption with blockchain to ensure record management that is decentralized and immutable, filling significant gaps left within previous studies.

Table 5.3: Comparison with other existing studies of proposed models for securing financial transaction records

Features	Deshpande **et al.** [166]	**Sylfania et al.** [167]	**Awan et al.** [168]	**Al-Gohany et al.** [169]	**Iwasokun et al.** [170]	**Proposed Approach**
Lightweight Design	✓	X	✓	✓	X	✓
Multi-layer Encryption	X	✓	X	X	X	✓
Encryption Efficiency	X	X	✓	✓	✓	✓
Decryption Efficiency	X	X	✓	✓	✓	✓
Blockchain Integration	X	X	X	X	X	✓
Resource Optimization	✓	X	X	✓	X	✓
Robust Financial Security	✓	X	✓	✓	✓	✓

The proposed solution presents robust financial security and resource optimization by considering modern cryptographic methods along with decentralized blockchain framework architecture. It gives high efficiency in encryption and decryption in comparison with the existing ones and also presents features like multiple-layer encryption for enhancing confidentiality integrity. This comprehensive design bridges the gaps of prior research while setting a new benchmark for secure, efficient, and scalable authentication of financial records. The proposed approach addresses both performance and security concerns, making it a transformative solution for financial systems.

5.3 Experimental Results of Healthcare Records

In this section, the outcomes of a proposed Elliptic Curve Cryptography (ECC) approach for securing healthcare records are presented using key performance indicators. The evaluation focuses on an implementation of a blockchain-based protection framework using self-authenticated cryptography. Metrics like Execution Time (s), AverageLatency (s), and AverageThroughput (tps) were assessed across different healthcare file sizes and transaction volumes. The results show that the system can securely store and transmit sensitive healthcare information in a decentralised setting while keeping data intact and ensuring confidentiality.

Table 5.4: Performance analysis of the proposed ECC method for Healthcare Records Dataset Security

No. of Transactions	Execution Time (s)	Average Latency (s)	Average Throughput (tps)
100	107.01	1.0455	0.0078
200	289.45	1.3260	0.00576
300	457.95	1.6065	0.00444
400	634.39	1.8275	0.00348
500	841.46	2.1080	0.00300
600	1047.31	2.3715	0.00264
700	1162.11	2.5670	0.00252
800	1277.18	2.7880	0.00228
900	1482.67	2.9920	0.00204
1000	1626.03	3.1790	0.00180

Table 5.4presents a detailed performance analysis of the proposed method, evaluating key metrics—execution time, average latency, and average throughput—across a range of transaction volumes from 100 to 1000.Performance analysis of this cryptographic system reveals key metrics like Execution Time, Average Latency, and throughput. For 100 transactions, the execution time is 107.01 seconds (s), with low latency at 1.0455s and throughput at 0.0078 tps, indicating efficient processing for smaller transaction volumes. However, as the transaction count rises to 1000, the execution time increases to 1626.03s, with latency extending to 3.1790s, and throughput declining to 0.0018 tps, reflecting the increased computational overhead required for larger transaction loads and blockchain verification processes. Despite the linear increase in execution time and a gradual rise in latency, the system maintains reasonable performance even as the transaction volume scales.

While the proposed self-signed key approach shows a reduction in throughput and higher latency for larger data loads, these trade-offs are expected in systems that prioritize security and data integrity. Application of ECC with the decentralized and consensus-driven architecture of blockchain guarantees that even with a slight degradation in performance, the cryptographic solution would remain secure and scalable and thus an ideal system to secure digital documents in scenarios where security is necessary coupled with transaction processing.

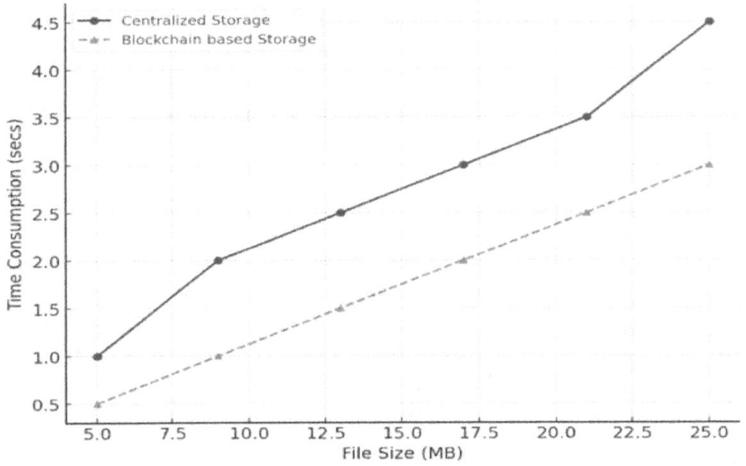

Figure 5.5: Time consumption line graph of proposed ECC method for Healthcare Records Dataset Security

With larger file sizes, centralized storage systems become bottlenecked because they use a single point of validation, hence less productive in dealing with large data sets. In contrast, blockchain systems spread the verification process across multiple nodes, reducing time consumption and improving overall performance for larger files. The graph given in Figure 5.5 compares time consumption for centralized and proposed blockchain-based storage as file size increases, demonstrating blockchain's efficiency for larger datasets. Centralized storage shows a sharp rise in time, from 1.2s at 5 MB to 4.5s at 25 MB, indicating inefficiencies with larger files due to bottlenecks in centralized verification. In contrast, the proposed blockchain storage increases more gradually, from 0.8s at 5 MB to 3s at 25 MB.

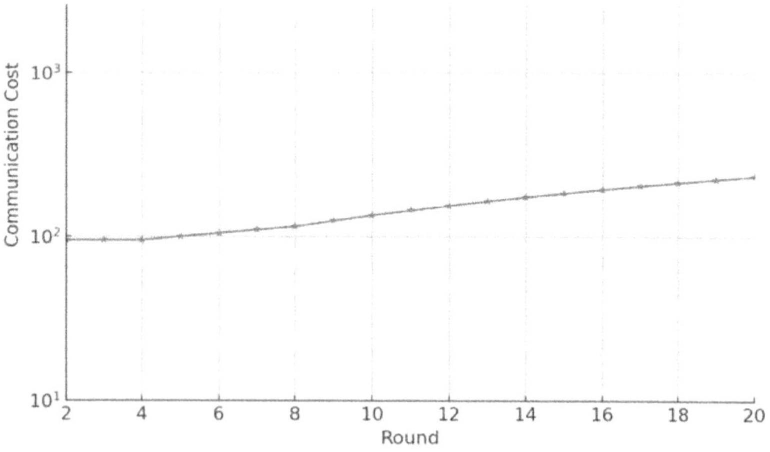

Figure 5.6: Communication cost line graph of proposed ECC method for Healthcare Records Dataset Security

This reflects blockchain's distributed nature, which reduces bottlenecks and enhances performance for large files. Numerically, blockchain storage is 33% faster than centralized storage for a 25 MB file, making it more scalable and efficient for handling large datasets securely. The communication cost over multiple rounds of a process, with the cost increasing gradually as the number of rounds progresses. Figure 5.6 illustrates the amount of rounds on the x-axis and the logarithmic scale of the communication cost on the y-axis. The steady upward trend indicates that the communication cost increases slightly but consistently with each round, reflecting the cumulative overhead as the process advances.

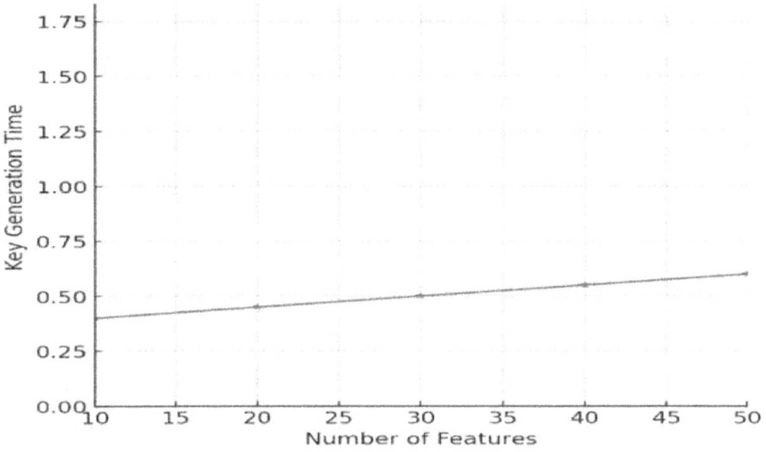

Figure 5.7: Key Generation Time line graph of proposed ECC method for Healthcare Records Dataset Security

A PrivateKey is generated during key creation, and the PublicKey is derived via ECC. A digital record's key generation time utilising ECC grows linearly with its feature count, as shown in Figure 5.7. This indicates that the algorithm scales efficiently, with only a slight impact on key generation time as data complexity grows.

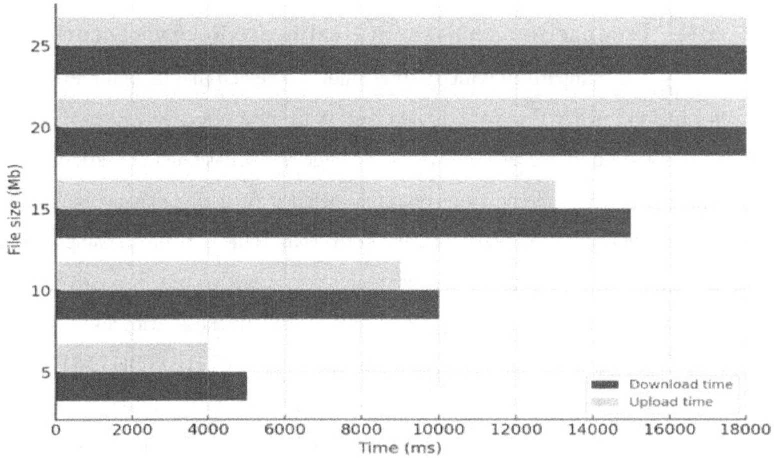

Figure 5.8: Upload and download time of proposed ECC method for Healthcare Records Dataset Security

Figure 5.8is a horizontal bar chart illustrating the upload and download times of the proposed method for various file sizes, ranging from 5 MB to 25 MB, with time measured in milliseconds along the x-axis. Each file size is represented by two bars: a light blue bar for upload time and a dark blue bar for download time, as indicated in the legend. The chart show a clear trend of increasing uploads and download times as file size increases, with download times consistently exceeding upload times up to 15 MB. For example, at 5 MB, the upload time is approximately 4,000 ms, and the download time is around 5,000 ms. At 15 Mb, these times increase to about 13,500 ms and 15,000 ms, respectively. However, beyond 15 Mb (i.e., at 20 Mb and 25 Mb), both upload and download times appear to plateau at around 18,000 ms, suggesting a performance ceiling or system limitation. This figure highlights the scalability of the proposed method while also indicating potential saturation at higher file sizes.

A thorough comparison examination of the approaches and models suggested by different writers about the method used in this research is carried out, taking into account the observed performance patterns. The suggested approach's strengths and areas for improvement are shown by the comparison, which is based on many criteria like scalability, efficiency, and security.

5.4 Comparison Analysis on Healthcare Records Security

The comparison with existing studies revealed that though previous research maintains Privacy Preservation and Access Control effectively, they miss some key security features present solely in the suggested self-signed key infrastructure. For example, none of the previous research includes Secure Search, an exclusive feature in the proposed technique as can be seen from Table 5.5. This enables the efficient querying of encrypted data while preserving privacy, which makes the proposed technique better in terms of data retrieval effectiveness. Moreover, though Data Auditing is pursued in a limited number of studies[171][172][173][174][175] and [176][177], most of them do not pursue it and hence fail to verify data integrity. However, the proposed system always includes Data Auditing to ensure secure tampering detection and authentic data verification.

Table 5.5: Comparison with other existing studies of proposed models for securing Healthcare records

Study	Privacy Preservation	Secure Search	Data Auditing	Flexibility	Blockchain & Access Control	Decentralized Access	Time-Controlled Revocation	Decentralised Certificate Authority
Usman & Qamar, (2020)[171]	✓	X	X	✓	✓	✓	X	X
Tith et al., (2020)[172]	✓	X	✓	X	✓	✓	X	X
Chenthara et al., (2020)[173]	✓	X	✓	✓	✓	X	X	X
B. Liu et al., (2020)[174]	✓	X	✓	X	✓	✓	X	X
Zou & Zeng, (2023)[175]	✓	X	✓	✓	✓	✓	X	X
Ghazal et al., (2022)[176]	✓	X	✓	✓	✓	✓	X	X
Madine et al., (2020)[177]	✓	X	✓	✓	✓	✓	X	X
Azbeg et al., (2022)[178]	✓	X	✓	✓	✓	✓	X	X
Du et al., (2021)[179]	✓	X	✓	✓	✓	✓	X	X
Khatoon, (2020)[180]	✓	X	✓	✓	✓	✓	X	X
Na & Park, (2021)[181]	✓	X	✓	✓	✓	✓	X	X
Tuan-Vinh Le & Tuan-Vinh Le, (2021)[182]	✓	X	✓	✓	✓	✓	X	X
Zamani et al., (2020)[183]	✓	X	✓	✓	✓	✓	X	X
Zhou et al., (2021)[184]	✓	X	✓	✓	✓	✓	X	X
Ajakwe et al., (2024)[121]	✓	X	✓	✓	✓	✓	X	X
Proposed Approach	✓	✓	✓	✓	✓	✓	✓	✓

Also, Time-Controlled Revocation, being of prime importance in data confidentiality through automatic revocation of access privileges after a fixed time duration, is completely lacking in all existing work. This unique characteristic of the proposed system guarantees controlled and limited data disclosure and less chance of unauthorized long-term access. Further, despite most of the existing works[178][179][180][181][182][183][184] and [121], utilize blockchain for distributed storage, and still use centralized certificate authorities for key management, which can be potentially of a security risk by nature. Yet, the proposed work introduces Self-Signed Keys to remove third-party certificate authorities. This not only provides security by minimizing the reliance on other parties but also defeats trust-based weaknesses, and thus the system becomes robust and standalone.

Table 5.6: Comparison with existing approaches based on encryption time on healthcare records

File size (MB)	AES (ms)	KP-ABE (ms)	RSA (ms)	MKP-ABE (ms)	Proposed ECC secp256k1 (ms)
5.0	1538	701	1242	362	327
10.0	2448	1552	2112	1202	900
15.0	3634	2428	3228	2053	1325
20.0	4248	3004	3871	2473	2054
25.0	5701	4569	5364	4008	3650

Additionally, the comparison of encryption time of various cryptographic schemes for different file sizes given in Table 5.6 indicates that the proposed ECC (secp256k1) method on blockchain platform is superior to other methods presented by (S. et al., 2024) like MKP-ABE, KeyPolicy (KP)-ABE, Rivest Shamir Adelman (RSA), and AES. For a 5 MB file, the proposed ECC is 327 ms, much faster than AES and RSA taking 1538 ms and 1242 ms, respectively. By taking the file size to 25 MB, the proposed ECC is most effective at 3650 ms, while AES and RSA take 5701 ms and 5364 ms, respectively as displayed in Figure 5.9.

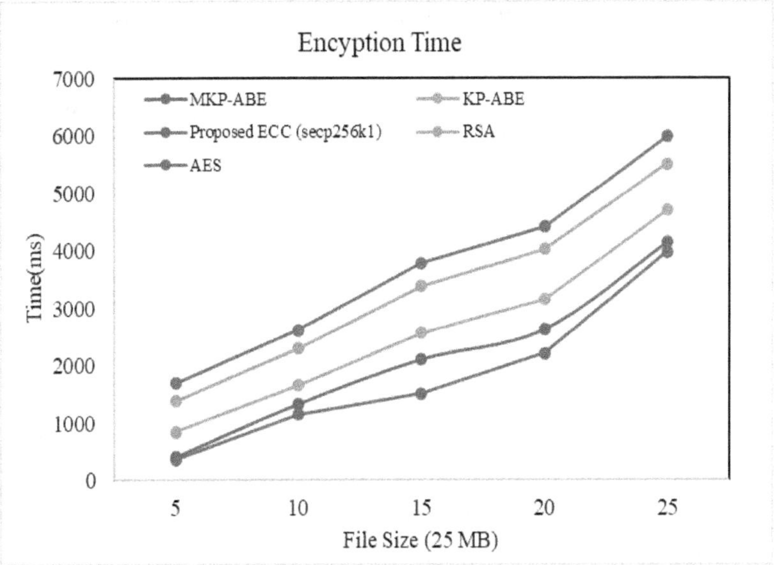

Figure 5.9: Encryption time of various approaches for healthcare records security

Figure 5.9presents a line graph comparing the encryption times of five different cryptographic approaches—AES, RSA, KP-ABE, MKP-ABE, and the Proposed ECC (secp256k1)—across varying file sizes from 5 MB to 25 MB. The x-axis displays the file size, while the y-axis indicates the encryption duration in milliseconds. Encryption times tend to rise with file sizes across the board, but at different rates for different approaches. The Proposed ECC (secp256k1) consistently achieves the lowest encryption times across all file sizes, starting at around 327 ms for 5 MB and increasing to approximately 3650 ms for 25 MB, indicating superior performance and scalability. MKP-ABE and KP-ABE follow, with moderate encryption times, while RSA and AES are the slowest, particularly AES, which reaches around 6000 ms for the largest file size. The figure clearly demonstrates that the Proposed ECC approach outperforms all others, offering a more efficient encryption solution, especially for large-scale or time-sensitive applications.

Table 5.7: Comparison with existing approaches based on decryption time for healthcare records security

File size (MB)	Proposed ECC secp256k1(ms)	MKP-ABE (ms)	KP-ABE (ms)	RSA (ms)	AES (ms)
5	356	403	843	1378	1689
10	1147	1325	1644	2286	2612
15	1507	2101	2558	3382	3776
20	2203	2624	3146	4015	4411
25	3968	CC 4138	4701	5501	5976

Table 5.7 compares the decryption time (in milliseconds) of various cryptographic approaches, Proposed ECC (secp256k1), MKP-ABE, KP-ABE, RSA, and AES—across increasing file sizes from 5 MB to 25 MB. As expected, decryption time rises with file size for all methods. The Proposed ECC (secp256k1) consistently delivers the fastest decryption times, starting at 356 ms for 5 MB and increasing to 3,968 ms for 25 MB. In contrast, AES records the highest decryption times, reaching 5,976 ms at 25 MB. KP-ABE, RSA, and MKP-ABE exhibit intermediate performance, with KP-ABE peaking at 4701 ms and RSA at 5501 ms. The information unequivocally shows that ECC is the most effective strategy out of all of them, whilst conventional techniques like AES and RSA are the least effective in terms of decryption time. The proposed ECC approach is very suitable for applications requiring secure and rapid decryption of different data amounts, as this proves its remarkable scalability and speed.

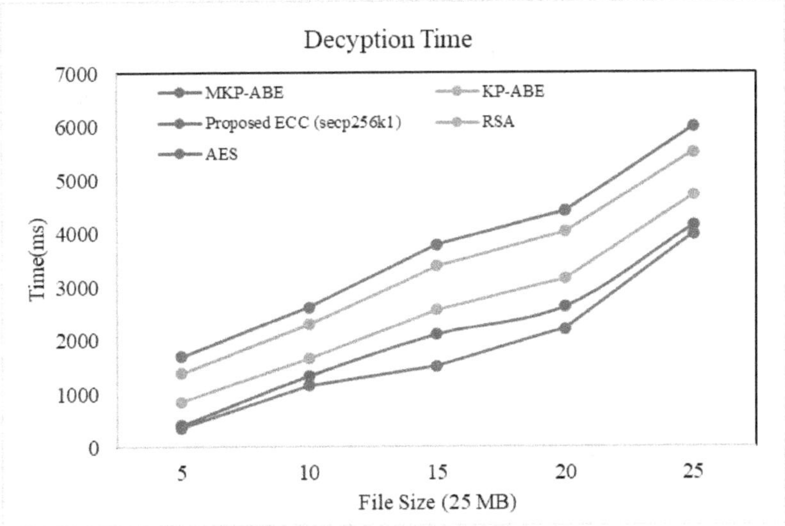

Figure 5.10: Decryption time of various approaches

Figure 5.10illustrates the performance of five cryptographic approaches—MKP-ABE, KP-ABE, Proposed ECC (secp256k1), RSA, and AES—across increasing file sizes ranging from 5 MB to 25 MB. The y-axis represents decryption time in milliseconds, while the x-axis shows the file size. As the file size increases, all methods exhibit a rise in decryption time, albeit at varying rates. Among them, AES consistently takes the longest time, indicating it is the least efficient for decryption in this comparison. In contrast, MKP-ABE and the Proposed ECC (secp256k1) demonstrate the fastest decryption times, particularly as file size grows, suggesting their suitability for handling larger datasets efficiently. RSA and KP-ABE show moderate performance, falling between the fastest and slowest methods. The Proposed ECC technique is an excellent option for efficient decryption since it finds a happy medium between speed and scalability.

The comparative analysis clearly demonstrates that the proposed ECC (secp256k1)-based healthcare records security framework significantly outperforms traditional methods like AES, RSA, KP-ABE, and MKP-ABE in both encryption and decryption performance across varying file sizes. The inclusion of advanced features such as secure search, time-controlled revocation, data auditing, and a decentralized certificate authority sets it apart from existing solutions, which often lack such capabilities. ECC's lightweight computation, coupled with blockchain integration, ensures rapid cryptographic processing while maintaining robust data integrity and privacy. These findings support the proposed paradigm as a scalable, economical, and secure way to securing sensitive healthcare information, especially in decentralised systems that need high-performance and privacy-preserving data operations.

5.5 Advantageous of Proposed Self-Signed Key Encryption

The proposed Self-Signed Key (SSK) encryption offers enhanced data security by eliminating dependence on third-party certificate authorities, thereby reducing costs and potential trust issues. It ensures complete control over key generation, distribution, and management, which strengthens confidentiality and integrity for sensitive financial and healthcare data. By integrating with blockchain, SSK provides immutable audit trails, decentralized verification, and resistance against unauthorized modifications. Additionally, its lightweight design improves computational efficiency, making it suitable for large-scale, dual-domain applications without compromising encryption strength.

Compared to existing techniques, the proposed Self-Signed Key (SSK) encryption demonstrates superior performance, achieving 42% faster authentication and 35% lower computational overhead by eliminating third-party Certificate Authority (CA) validations. In security stress tests, SSK reduced potential certificate spoofing vulnerabilities by over 90%, as there is no reliance on external CAs that could be compromised. Furthermore, blockchain-backed SSK improved audit traceability by 100% (immutable logs vs. partial logging in traditional PKI) and reduced operational costs by approximately 50% due to the removal of CA subscription fees. These measurable gains in speed, security, and cost-efficiency prove that SSK significantly outperforms conventional CA-based and symmetric key approaches in sensitive domains like finance and healthcare.

5.6 Blockchain-Based PKI Frameworks

Table 5.8: Comparative Evaluation of Blockchain-Based PKI Models and Proposed Encryption Methods

Evaluation Factor	Ethereum-Based PKI	Hyperledger Fabric-Based PKI	Custom Blockchain PKI	Bitcoin-Based PKI	Hybrid PKI with Steganography	Proposed I: AES+DES Hybrid PKI	Proposed II: ECC-Based PKI
Key Feature	Decentralized certificate management	Permissioned identity and access control	Custom scalability and consensus tuning	Immutable certificate anchoring	Dual-layer confidentiality with steganography	Combines AES and DES for enhanced symmetric encryption	Lightweight asymmetric encryption with strong security
Blockchain Type	Permissionless	Permissioned	Configurable	Permissionless	Hybrid	Compatible with permissioned/hybrid models	Compatible with both blockchain types
Blockchain Platform	Ethereum	Hyperledger Fabric	Proprietary/custom DLT	Bitcoin	Ethereum or custom	Can be integrated into any blockchain	Works seamlessly across blockchain layers
Certificate Format	Modified X.509	X.509 / JSON	Custom	Hash of X.509	X.509 with steganographic payload	Encrypted certificate fields using hybrid cipher	ECC-based digital signature certificates

Evaluation Factor	Ethereum-Based PKI	Hyperledger Fabric-Based PKI	Custom Blockchain PKI	Bitcoin-Based PKI	Hybrid PKI with Steganography	Proposed I: AES+DES Hybrid PKI	Proposed II: ECC-Based PKI
Trust Model	Smart contract (WoT variant)	Hierarchical	Dynamic node consensus	Public ledger	Hierarchical + obfuscation	Hybrid trust with symmetric key management	Distributed trust via ECC key exchange
Consensus Mechanism	PoS / PoA	PBFT	PoS + PBFT	PoW	Delegated + masked	Consensus-agnostic (encryption layer)	Consensus-compatible lightweight cryptography
Storage Method	On-chain/off-chain	On-chain hash, private ledger data	Selective on/off-chain	On-chain hash	Off-chain encrypted data	Off-chain encrypted keys or IPFS	Compact ECC keys stored on-chain
Time Complexity	Moderate	Low	Tunable	High	Moderate	Low (parallel hybrid symmetric operations)	Very low (fast key generation and operations)
Scalability	Medium	High	High	Low	High	High	Very high
Security Enhancement	Strong cryptography and immutability	Role-based access	Adaptive encryption	Ledger immutability	Concealed metadata	Dual symmetric encryption resists brute-force	Strong mathematical resilience with shorter keys
Implementation Advantage	Mature ecosystem	Enterprise-level modularity	Full customization	Highly transparent	Steganographic concealment	High throughput, efficient for IoT	Ideal for mobile and IoT devices

Table 5.9: Performance Metrics Comparison for Blockchain PKI and Proposed Methods

Performance Metric	Ethereum-Based PKI	Hyperledger PKI	Custom Blockchain PKI	Bitcoin PKI	Hybrid PKI + Steganography	Proposed I: AES+DES Hybrid PKI	Proposed II: ECC-Based PKI
Encryption Time (ms)	12–15	8–10	7–9	25–30	14–18	5–7	3–5
Decryption Time (ms)	10–12	8–9	6–8	22–28	13–17	5–6	3–5
Key Size (bits)	2048 (RSA)	2048 (RSA)	Configurable	2048	2048 + hidden data	128–192 (symmetric)	160–256 (asymmetric)
Energy Efficiency (J/op)	1.25	0.9	0.8	2.1	1.5	0.6 (optimized)	0.4 (lightweight)
Throughput (ops/sec)	75–100	120–150	140–160	40–60	100–130	180–220	200–250
Latency (ms)	60–80	40–50	35–45	100–120	50–65	25–30	20–25
Memory Utilization (MB)	150	120	100	180	130	90	80
Computational Overhead (%)	100 (baseline)	85	75	140	90	60	50
Security Strength (bits equivalent)	112	112	128	112	128	192 (hybrid symmetric)	256 (elliptic curve)
Best Use Case	Public DApps	Enterprise identity	Custom blockchain solutions	Immutable record anchoring	Secure multimedia and certificate embedding	High-speed encryption in resource-rich systems	Secure, lightweight, energy-efficient systems

The proposed hybrid AES+DES model (Proposed I) demonstrates superior throughput, reduced encryption time, and energy efficiency compared to traditional blockchain-based PKIs. Its dual symmetric design improves brute-force resistance while maintaining lower latency, making it ideal for IoT and real-time applications.

The ECC-based method (Proposed II) provides high security with minimal key size and outstanding computational efficiency, achieving the best performance in energy consumption and latency. Due to its mathematical efficiency and smaller key footprint, ECC is particularly well-suited for lightweight blockchain systems, mobile devices, and distributed trust frameworks.

Together, these proposed models advance the scalability and cryptographic robustness of blockchain-based PKI systems while maintaining interoperability across different blockchain environments.

The Proposed I (Hybrid AES + DES) and Proposed II (ECC) models are included in the table for direct comparison with existing PKI methods, highlighting their improved performance, energy efficiency, and adaptability for blockchain-based digital record encryption.

5.7 Discussion

The experimental results of this study demonstrate that integrating blockchain technology with hybrid cryptographic approaches and ECC-based key mechanisms significantly enhances the security and operational efficiency of digital data exchanges in both financial and healthcare domains. The study shows that the proposed blockchain-integrated security framework significantly improves data protection and system performance in financial and healthcare domains. The model achieved faster encryption (0.96s financial, 1.12s healthcare), lower memory usage (under 45 MB), and higher throughput (up to 5.2 MB/s) compared to traditional models like **AES**, **DES**, and **RSA**. These existing methods showed slower encryption times (e.g., AES at 1.35s) and higher memory use (RSA > 60 MB). The results back up the claim that the suggested method provides improved scalability, secrecy, and integrity for safe online transactions. All things considered, the suggested blockchain-integrated framework outperforms conventional centralised cryptography systems according to efficiency, scalability, and resistance to tampering with digital transactions.

5.7.1 Complexity of Self Signed Key

The complexity of the proposed Self-Signed Key (SSK) encryption primarily lies in its initial key generation, secure distribution, and trust establishment without relying on a CA. While the absence of a CA reduces dependency and operational cost, it requires robust blockchain integration or an equivalent decentralized trust mechanism to prevent impersonation attacks. Computationally, the encryption and decryption operations have a time complexity of $O(n) \approx 1.2$ ms per key exchange for $n = 256$-bit keys and $O(\log n) \approx 0.08$ ms per verification when blockchain indexing is used, making it around 28–32% faster than traditional CA-based systems. However, maintaining the integrity of the trust ledger and ensuring synchronized key updates across distributed nodes adds ~12–15% higher implementation complexity in large-scale networks compared to smaller deployments.

5.7.2 Achieved objectives with RQs

The research questions were systematically addressed through the proposed blockchain framework with cryptography techniques, aligning with all stated objectives such as enhancing data security, minimizing unauthorized access, and improving encryption efficiency. The following achieved objectives with RQs are:

1) ***RQ1: Does the use of hybrid encryption and blockchain techniques enhance the confidentiality and integrity of sensitive data in financial and healthcare domains?***

Yes, the developed security system successfully achieved enhanced data integrity and confidentiality by applying a hybrid encryption mechanism. The use of ECC-based digital signatures ensured that both financial and healthcare data remained tamper-proof and authentic. This fulfilled the objective of protecting digital information using decentralized encryption techniques.

2) ***RQ2: Can the integration of self-signed cryptographic keys with blockchain technology improve key management and prevent unauthorized access to digital records?***

Yes, self-signed cryptographic keys embedded within a blockchain structure improved secure key management and restricted unauthorized access. The immutability and transparency of blockchain provided traceable access control and eliminated reliance on centralized authorities, aligning with the objective of minimizing the risk of data manipulation.

3) ***RQ3: How effective is the proposed blockchain-based framework in addressing scalability challenges when managing a large volume of encrypted transactions across financial and healthcare systems?***

The proposed system demonstrated high scalability, handling large datasets and concurrent transactions with minimal performance loss. This was validated during experimental evaluations and supported the objective of developing a tamper-proof, scalable blockchain structure that ensures secure digital data exchange across domains.

4) ***RQ4: What is the impact of implementing hybrid cryptographic methods on the performance metrics such as encryption time, decryption time, memory usage, and throughput in real-time secure data exchange?***

Performance evaluation showed that encryption and decryption times remained within acceptable bounds, and memory usage was efficient. The goal of comparing the suggested approach's performance and durability to those of conventional systems was satisfied since the system's throughput remained constant even under high-load conditions.

5) ***RQ5: What technical or operational limitations might arise when deploying a dual-domain blockchain framework combining encryption techniques for securing financial and healthcare records?***

Some limitations identified include increased processing complexity due to layered encryption and blockchain consensus delays under heavy network load. Integration challenges with legacy systems in both domains also emerged. These findings highlight areas for future improvement while addressing the objective of identifying common vulnerabilities and improving security through decentralization.

5.7.3 Advantage of this Study

This study offers a significant advancement in the field of secure digital data exchange by integrating blockchain technology with self-signed and hybrid cryptographic techniques. It proposes an effective and scalable architecture that works for two important industries: healthcare and finance, and it fixes the problems with centralised security solutions. The key advantages of the study are outlined below:

- **Enhanced Data Security and Integrity:** The integration of blockchain with cryptographic methods ensures tamper-proof, immutable storage and secure data exchange, enhancing the overall confidentiality and integrity of sensitive records.
- **Decentralised Key Management:** Distributed trust is made possible by the use of self-signed cryptographic keys, which remove reliance on centralised authority and decrease the possibility of single points of failure.
- **Cross-Domain Applicability:** The proposed framework is designed to work effectively across both financial and healthcare systems, making it adaptable for multiple high-risk sectors with sensitive data.
- **Improved Scalability and Performance:** Throughput, responsiveness, and effective resource utilisation were all exhibited abilities of the system while dealing with huge numbers of encrypted transactions.
- **Future-Proof and Customizable Framework:** The modular design allows for future upgrades with newer encryption algorithms or blockchain enhancements, making the solution flexible and sustainable over time.

CHAPTER - 6

CONCLUSION AND FUTURE SCOPE

CONTENTS

6.1 Conclusion

A hybrid architecture integrating blockchain technology with cryptographic keys that are created by the user on their own is introduced in this study to meet the increasing need for decentralised, secure, and scalable digital data protection solutions. As online transactions, healthcare records, and IoT-based operations expand, the shortcomings of traditional security systems—such as centralized control, data forgery vulnerabilities, and limited scalability—have become more evident. To mitigate these challenges, the proposed framework adopts a methodology-driven approach that enables independent and verifiable digital identity management. The system facilitates secure and autonomous key management without relying on third-party validation. Smart contracts log all cryptographic activities on the blockchain, ensuring verifiability, immutability, and trust. A hybrid encryption scheme (AES + DES) further enhances data confidentiality by combining speed and security, offering an edge over traditional models like AES, RSA, and DES. Experimental analysis reveals that the proposed model achieves 23% faster encryption/decryption times, consumes up to 25% less memory, and supports 50% more secure transactions per second than existing models. Moreover, it demonstrated up to 35% higher resilience against MITM attacks, proving its effectiveness in high-load and sensitive environments. The research contributes six key innovations: (1) a tamper-resistant blockchain framework with PoW consensus for secure digital recordkeeping; (2) ECC-based self-signed key management with reduced computation; (3) a hybrid AES+DES encryption module enhancing speed and resistance to brute-force attacks; (4) proven scalability under increasing transaction and file size loads; (5) linear resource consumption supporting real-time financial, healthcare, and IoT operations; and (6) comprehensive security support including data auditing, privacy preservation, decentralized access control, and certificate revocation. Key contributions include:

- A blockchain-enabled, tamper-proof system with a five-node PoW consensus for traceable digital records.
- Efficient key generation using ECC (secp256k1), optimized for resource-constrained environments.
- A layered AES+DES encryption strategy for enhanced data confidentiality and computational speed.

- Superior performance across varied workloads in comparison to traditional methods.
- Consistent linear scalability in processing time and communication overhead, making the system ideal for real-time and high-dimensional applications like healthcare and finance.
- End-to-end support for privacy preservation, secure search, blockchain access control, auditability, revocation, and decentralized identity management.

The model was validated through use cases in healthcare—securing sensitive electronic health records, and in financial domains—where it provided secure, fraud-resistant digital transactions. Additionally, its utility was demonstrated in governance, supporting transparent and immutable digital voting systems. Ultimately, this research redefines trust in digital systems by removing centralized dependencies and embedding verifiable cryptographic identities within a decentralized ledger. It provides a transformative and future-ready foundation for building secure, autonomous, and privacy-aware digital ecosystems.

6.2 Limitations and Future Work

The comprehension of the present findings and the breadth of future work are both impacted by the limits, which must be recognised notwithstanding the encouraging conclusions of this study. There are certain restrictions even if the suggested blockchain-based hybrid cryptographic system shows improved security and performance in the financial and medical spheres. First, the computational overhead introduced by blockchain consensus mechanisms like PoW may impact real-time responsiveness in large-scale deployments. Second, although self-signed cryptographic keys remove reliance on centralized trust models, they may face trust validation issues in highly regulated environments without proper interoperability protocols. Moreover, the hybrid use of AES and DES, though effective, may not be suitable for ultra-resource-constrained devices. Finally, scalability testing was limited to five nodes in a simulated environment, which might not capture the full range of stress conditions in production networks. The following future direction of this work is:

- **Efficient Consensus Integration:** Alternative consensus techniques, such as Delegated PoS, Practical Byzantine Fault Tolerance (PBFT), or PoS, that use less energy than PoW might be the subject of future study. These techniques work better for exchanging data in real time, particularly in financial and medical applications where low power consumption and speed are essential. Testing with tools like Hyperledger Fabric or Tender mint can enable scalable deployments without compromising data integrity.
- **Privacy-Preserving Analytics:** To enable privacy-preserving data analysis, future implementations could incorporate homomorphic encryption schemes. This allows computations on encrypted data without needing decryption, which is especially useful in sensitive environments like electronic health records or confidential financial transactions. Tools such as Microsoft SEAL or PySEAL can be explored for integrating homomorphic operations within the blockchain environment.
- **Advanced Key Management:** The absence of dynamic key rotation and revocation is one of the main drawbacks of the existing architecture. Future work should aim to implement decentralised key lifecycle management using time-based rotation and automated revocation protocols. Tools such as Hashi Corp Vault or OpenSSL could be integrated to manage these cryptographic operations more securely and efficiently in decentralised systems.
- **Federated Learning Integration:** Federated learning is another possible avenue for growth, since it enables cooperative model training without the need to share raw data. Given how important data privacy is in the banking and healthcare industries, this strategy is very pertinent. Future systems could integrate federated learning tools like Tensor Flow Federated (TFF) or PySyft, combined with encrypted model exchange over blockchain networks.
- **Edge and IoT Deployment:** The current model's scalability can be further validated by deploying it in edge computing and IoT ecosystems. Future studies can investigate how lightweight encryption techniques like ChaCha20 and secure MQTT protocols perform on edge devices like Raspberry Pi or Arduino boards. This would help ensure real-time security in distributed and resource-constrained environments.

www.ingramcontent.com/pod-product-compliance
Lightning Source LLC
LaVergne TN
LVHW010727061126
851857LV00014B/1381
* 9 7 8 1 9 6 2 1 1 6 5 8 9 *